walking san Francisco

WALKING SAN FRANCISCO

30 savvy tours
exploring steep streets,
grand hotels, dive bars,
and waterfront parks

Tom Downs

WILDERNESS PRESS · BERKELEY, CA

Walking San Francisco: 30 savvy tours exploring steep streets, grand hotels, dive bars, and waterfront parks

1st EDITION July 2007
  2nd printing May 2008

Cover photos copyright © 2007 by Tom Downs, except for the following by Larry B. Van Dyke: front cover, top center; all photos on back cover.
Interior photos: Tom Downs, except for following: Roslyn Bullas, pp. 137 & 173; Larry B. Van Dyke, pp. 13, 63, 199, & 201.
Maps: Bart Wright/Lohnes + Wright
Book and cover design: Larry B. Van Dyke
Book production: Lisa Pletka
Book editor: Elaine Merrill

ISBN 978-0-89997-419-4
UPC 7-19609-97419-2

Manufactured in China

Published by: **Wilderness Press**
               1200 5th Street
               Berkeley, CA 94710
               (800) 443-7227; FAX (510) 558-1696
               info@wildernesspress.com
               www.wildernesspress.com

Visit our website for a complete listing of our books and for ordering information.

Cover photos: *Front, clockwise from bottom center:* Doc's Clock, Mission District; City Hall, Civic Center; Diego Rivera's fresco, Russian Hill; pagoda-style architecture, Chinatown; Washington Square Park, North Beach; Haas-Lilienthal House, Pacific Heights; Willie McCovey statue, China Park Basin. *Back, clockwise from bottom left:* City Lights Bookstore and Transamerica Pyramid; Crissy Field; New May Wah, Richmond District.
Frontispiece: Golden Gate Bridge from the Presidio.

SAFETY NOTICE: Although Wilderness Press and the author have made every attempt to ensure that the information in this book is accurate at press time, they are not responsible for any loss, damage, injury, or inconvenience that may occur to anyone while using this book. You are responsible for your own safety and health while following the walking trips described here. Always check local conditions, know your own limitations, and consult a map.

acknowledgments

My partners in crime are people who have shared their knowledge and interests with me, usually over turkey sandwiches at Lefty's or beers in places like the Ha Ra and the Uptown. Some even walked with me. They include Beca Lafore, John Fadeff, Chris Harris, Mark Carrodus, Jim Downs, Randall Homan, Al Barna, Rob Browne, Ryan Ver Berkmoes, and Fawn Downs. I'd also like to thank publishing manager Roslyn Bullas, editor Elaine Merrill, designers Larry Van Dyke and Lisa Pletka, and cartographer Bart Wright.

author's note

Apart from good shoes, the most important thing you'll want to bring along for these walks is a healthy sense of curiosity. No matter where you walk, whether it's in a city or in a natural setting, you're bound to wonder about the places you're walking through. That may involve trying to identify a type of architecture or a type of bird. For me, especially in cities, that interest always extends beyond the surface, and often into the past. I like to know what's going on in the places where I walk, and also what has gone on there before. Things are always changing, but the past is never completely obliterated. We can see the buildings, remember the stories. In that sense, these walks can be taken as grab bags of anecdotes and trivia all tied to a patch of geography known as San Francisco. They are also appreciations of a beautiful city.

While walking, use all the common sense you would usually have while strolling the streets of an American city. This book covers a lot of ground, and is not limited to the hoitiest neighborhoods. That said, the only truly gritty district we'll walk through is the Tenderloin. Some parts of the Mission District also have their share of crime, but usually at night.

Perhaps the greatest caution should be exercised while doing the two bar-hopping tours in this book. On these walks, if you're not in your right mind, you're likely to stroll in front of a moving vehicle—or get shanghaied or something. Keep your wits about you, don't drink more than you can handle, and you'll be OK.

Alright. Walk on.

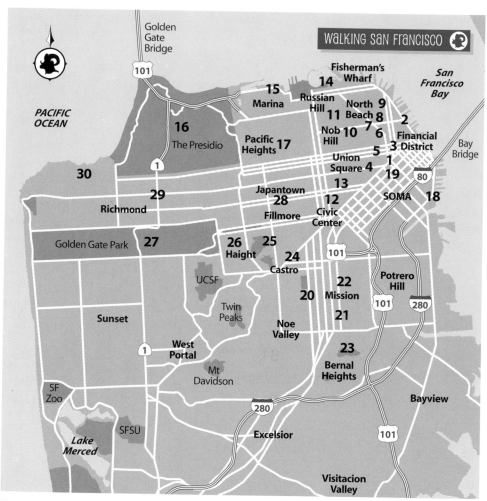

Numbers on this locator map correspond to Walk numbers.

acknowledgments

My partners in crime are people who have shared their knowledge and interests with me, usually over turkey sandwiches at Lefty's or beers in places like the Ha Ra and the Uptown. Some even walked with me. They include Beca Lafore, John Fadeff, Chris Harris, Mark Carrodus, Jim Downs, Randall Homan, Al Barna, Rob Browne, Ryan Ver Berkmoes, and Fawn Downs. I'd also like to thank publishing manager Roslyn Bullas, editor Elaine Merrill, designers Larry Van Dyke and Lisa Pletka, and cartographer Bart Wright.

author's note

Apart from good shoes, the most important thing you'll want to bring along for these walks is a healthy sense of curiosity. No matter where you walk, whether it's in a city or in a natural setting, you're bound to wonder about the places you're walking through. That may involve trying to identify a type of architecture or a type of bird. For me, especially in cities, that interest always extends beyond the surface, and often into the past. I like to know what's going on in the places where I walk, and also what has gone on there before. Things are always changing, but the past is never completely obliterated. We can see the buildings, remember the stories. In that sense, these walks can be taken as grab bags of anecdotes and trivia all tied to a patch of geography known as San Francisco. They are also appreciations of a beautiful city.

While walking, use all the common sense you would usually have while strolling the streets of an American city. This book covers a lot of ground, and is not limited to the hoitiest neighborhoods. That said, the only truly gritty district we'll walk through is the Tenderloin. Some parts of the Mission District also have their share of crime, but usually at night.

Perhaps the greatest caution should be exercised while doing the two bar-hopping tours in this book. On these walks, if you're not in your right mind, you're likely to stroll in front of a moving vehicle—or get shanghaied or something. Keep your wits about you, don't drink more than you can handle, and you'll be OK.

Alright. Walk on.

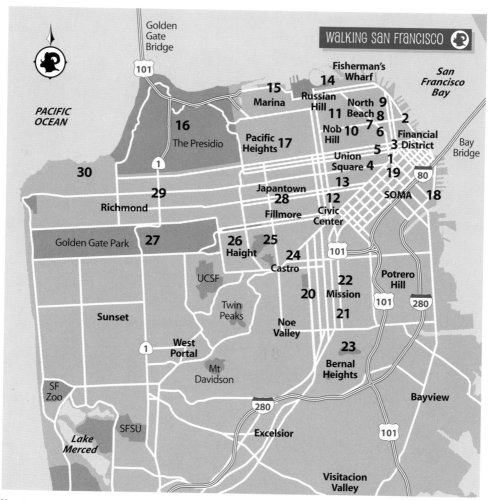

Numbers on this locator map correspond to Walk numbers.

TABLE OF CONTENTS

INTRODUCTION

San Francisco is a great walking city. It's a city of distinct neighborhoods, each with an intriguing history, beautiful buildings, and inviting places to eat or drink. That the city is far from flat may deter some, but rarely does San Francisco require a walker to trek up more than two steep blocks. Besides, reaching the top always has its obvious rewards, for the city's renowned beauty is fully realized only from the crest of its hills.

Most San Franciscans are accustomed to walking their city, but even city dwellers tend to have their familiar routes, which take them to where they need to go on a daily basis. This book invites locals and visitors to broaden their horizons, to explore well-trodden sidewalks at a slower pace, and to venture off into the hidden corners of the city. These are not purposeful walks, but meandering, inquisitive strolls that focus on the story behind the buildings, the details that are easily missed if you're moving too fast, the unexpected detours down narrow alleys and into unassuming shops where surprises await. The philosophy of this book is that the pleasure is in getting there.

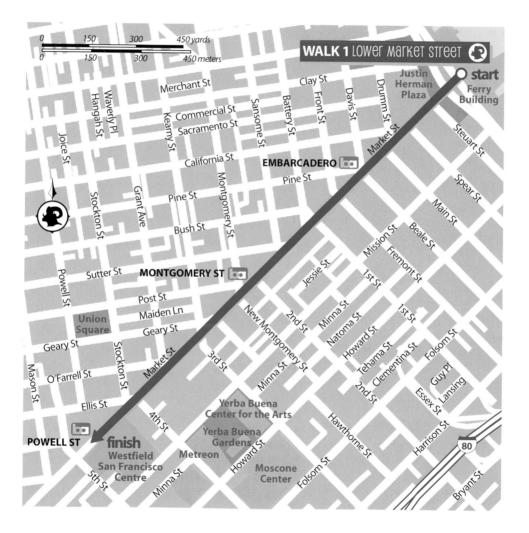

1 LOWER MARKET STREET: WHEELIN' AND DEALIN' DOWN SF'S MAIN STREET

BOUNDARIES: Market St. from the Embarcadero to Powell St.
DISTANCE: 1¼ miles
DIFFICULTY: Easy
PARKING: There's a parking garage at Embarcadero 2.
PUBLIC TRANSIT: F streetcars (street level); J, K, L, M, N and S streetcars (underground);
  Embarcadero BART; 1, 2, 7, 14, 21, and 71 Muni

Market St. slices through San Francisco's grid at a brash, oblique angle, cutting a prominent seam through the city's central neighborhoods. Indeed, it was laid out to be a grand boulevard. It doesn't always live up to the billing, particularly in the Civic Center area, where many of the shop fronts are boarded up, but this tour will focus on the most historic and thriving part of Market St., from the Embarcadero to Powell St. To walk this graceful corridor on a weekday morning is to be urged along by the living thrum of an American city. Muni buses, taxis, restored streetcars, autos, and bicycles generate a deep-throated hush as their wheels roll up and down Market's lanes. The street's swift-footed office workers swerve to avoid statues, fountains, and historical markers, as well as the casual sightseer who stops to inspect these monuments of the street's stately past. Billions in U.S. dollars have been earned, lost, and swindled in the high-rise and flat iron structures along this, the city's main thoroughfare.

● Start at the foot of Market St., where it nearly meets the Embarcadero. The open space here is Justin Herman Plaza, named for the controversial head of San Francisco's Redevelopment Agency who served from 1959 to 1971. (Herman is generally held accountable for the displacement of thousands of black residents in the Western Addition, as that neighborhood was subjected to extensive renewal projects during the early 1960s.) For decades, this awkward plaza was marred by the elevated Embarcadero Freeway, which ran along the bayfront until the 1989 Loma Prieta earthquake brought it down. Today the plaza is a pleasant space, with palm trees, an open-air crafts market, and live music several days a week around lunchtime. At the plaza's northeastern corner is homely Villaincourt Fountain, described by the late *San*

Francisco Chronicle architecture critic Allan Temko as something "deposited by a concrete dog with square intestines." Inspecting the fountain more closely may make you feel like a concrete fly. Nevertheless, steps through the fountain's shallow pool invite you to venture behind the huge spouts, where you're likely to get a wee bit wet while enjoying a backstage perspective. This is a good vantage of the staggered backside of the Hyatt Regency Hotel. (The Embarcadero Center, which also towers over the plaza, is included in Walk No. 3, the Financial District.)

● Start up Market St., noting the attractive One Market building across the street. It was home base for the Southern Pacific Railroad, the enormous conglomerate run by the Big Four railroad magnates, who dominated transportation in the Western U.S. during the late 19th century. The building went up in 1916. SP, as the railroad was known to hobos and train spotters, survived until 1996, when the company was absorbed by Union Pacific.

● At Drumm St., turn right and enter the Hyatt Regency, which is merely interesting from the outside, but looks truly spectacular from within. Head up the escalator to the Atrium level, where glass elevators whiz up to tiered, vertigo-inducing balconies. Mel Brooks took full advantage of the striking setting when he shot scenes for *High Anxiety* here. Ride an elevator up and down and get back to Market St.

● Cross at Spear, toward the sidewalk flower stand designed to look like a Muni bus. The high loggia arching halfway over the sidewalk here is part of the Federal Reserve Bank, completed in 1983. Inside, exhibits explore the theme of money and banking; you'll see a currency collection dating back to colonial days.

● The next block is dominated by the Matson and PG&E buildings, which make a perfect pair. The Matson office, home to the city's largest shipping line, was built in 1921, and the office of the local power company, PG&E, went up four years later. Scan the ledges of the upper floors of these buildings and you might spot one of the peregrine falcons that regularly perch there. From 2003–05, two falcons, dubbed Gracie and George, raised their nestlings outside the 33rd floor of the PG&E Building, overlooking Beale St. They've since moved across the street, and they and their offspring are still often seen amid the high-rises of Market St.

- If you look back across Market St., you'll get an eyeful of 101 California St., a cylindrical glass tower that's worth a closer look. Cross over to it, and you'll see that the lower floors are supported by unclad pillars. The exposed pillars, which of course continue unseen to the top of the building, look naked and suspiciously vulnerable without the glass curtain. Unfortunately, 101 California is known mostly as the scene of a senseless murder-suicide. On July 1, 1993, John Luigi Ferri, a disgruntled claimant, entered the law offices of Pettit & Martin, on the 34th floor, and gunned down eight employees before killing himself. Six others were wounded in the attack.

- At the confluence of Market, Battery, and Bush streets, breaking office workers and bike messengers often perch at the base of the Mechanics statue, a robust bronze by Douglas Tilden, who was educated at San Francisco's Deaf and Dumb and Blind Asylum. (He was deaf.) The statue was unveiled in 1901 to some protest from those who observed that the subjects—muscular ironworkers—were not wearing pants beneath their blacksmith aprons, leaving their bums exposed to the elements. Tilden himself, regarded as the Michelangelo of the West, argued he was observing the classical ideal. The nude ironworkers may have had their hams roasted during the 1906 quake and fire, but were otherwise little harmed.

- Midway across Battery, on the little triangular island, keep your eyes peeled for a historical marker that informs us the slot machine was invented by Charles August Fey in his workshop near this spot in 1894. For the better part of a century, Fey's three-reel, hand-cranked "one-armed bandit" was the slot machine of choice in many a Nevada casino. The green-tinted glass curtain wall that towers over the next block (between Battery

Hyatt Regency

Back Story: Palatial Intrigue

The original Palace Hotel was the center of the city's social life and the downfall of William Ralston, the banker who literally went belly up while building it. First Ralston went bankrupt and then he died while swimming in the bay a few weeks before the hotel's opening. Many suspect it was a suicide.

Three decades later, opera star Enrico Caruso, in town to perform in a production of *Carmen,* stayed in the old Palace the night of April 17, 1906. Just after 5 a.m. the following morning, Caruso evacuated the shaking building several hours before flames engulfed it. Some eye-witnesses claimed the singer was in an embarrassing state of panic, but Caruso wrote a lengthy account for a London publication refuting this attack on his charac-

ter. He admitted he and his valet wandered helplessly about the city, as did thousands of others, while the entire downtown area went up in smoke. He slept on the ground on the night of April 18 and found his way out of town the following day. He never returned to San Francisco.

On August 2, 1923, President Warren G. Harding—rated by some historians as the worst president in U.S. history—died at the rebuilt Palace Hotel after he was stricken with food poisoning while sailing to the city from Alaska. Mysteriously, no one Harding had dined with got sick, and conspiracy theories abound. (Historian Robert H. Ferrell has concluded, not to everybody's satisfaction, that the president died of a heart attack.)

and Sansome) is the Crown Zellerbach Building. Built in 1959, it's one of San Francisco's most attractive modern buildings.

- The triangular corners of Market St. have necessitated the design of numerous flat-iron buildings, so called because they are shaped like the old blockish irons long ago heated on stoves before being applied to wrinkled shirts. Modern office towers such as the Crown Zellerbach Building often flout the shape of their lots with surrounding plazas and whatnot, but the next block is occupied by a traditional flatiron building of the sort that once lined much of Market St. This tasteful flatiron dates to 1913.

- On the same block, toward the wider end, stands the Hobart Building, an attractive 1914 Willis Polk design. Part of the building's unintended appeal comes from the fact that its design took a shorter adjacent neighbor into account. When that building was demolished and replaced by an even shorter structure, the Hobart Building's flat western flank was awkwardly exposed. In any case, it's still lovely to look at.

- Cross Market St. and glance back for a better perspective of the Hobart Building before heading half a block up New Montgomery to the main entrance of the Palace Hotel. It was built in 1909 on the site of the far more magnificent original Palace, which was destroyed by the '06 conflagration. The Palace is still spectacular, especially the interior garden court with its stunningly beautiful glass roof. Go inside for a look, or for an expensive pot of tea, and exit via a hall leading back to Market St. On your way out, you'll pass the Pied Piper bar. If it's open, peek inside for a look at the mural by Maxfield Parrish. If you're a mite parched you can stop for a beer as well. (An inviting alternative for a drink or decent bar food would be House of Shields, a great old tavern on New Montgomery, across from the Palace Hotel's main entrance.)

- Another block up, at the corner of 3rd and Market, is the Hearst Building, its entry marked by a big "H." Built in 1909, it was home to William Randolph Hearst's *San Francisco Examiner.* Julia Morgan designed the building's Baroque entry, which was added in 1937. This intersection was home to two of the city's other leading papers during the early 20th century, with the *Call* and *Chronicle* occupying opposing corners. The Chronicle Tower (690 Market St) and the once glorious Call Building have been remodeled beyond recognition and there's little to suggest reporters once bustled through their doors.

- Across Market from the Hearst Building you'll spot Lotta's Fountain, legendary for the congregations that gather here every year on April 18 to commemorate the 1906 earthquake. The festivities traditionally include a few quake survivors, whose numbers are obviously dwindling. In the aftermath of the quake, the fountain was a meeting place for separated families. It was a gift to the city in 1875 from Lotta Crabtree (1847–1924), a beguiling redhead who as a child entertainer worked the halls of Sierra Nevada mining towns. When she matured she moved East and became the "Belle of Broadway."

- At the intersection of Market, Grant, and O'Farrell streets is the Phelan Building, a large and elegant flatiron. Clad in white terra-cotta tiles, it's one of the prettiest sights on all of Market St. James Duvall Phelan, the city's mayor from 1897 to 1903 and a U.S. Senator from 1913 to 1919, kept his offices here after the building went up in 1908.

- The next block is dominated by the grey hulk of the Flood Building, built by James L. Flood, son of the silver king James C. Flood. It's an impressive eye-catcher with a staunch demeanor. In the early 1920s, Dashiell Hammett, yet to establish himself as the father of American crime fiction, worked upstairs for the local branch of the Pinkerton Detective Agency. Today, as you'll see, its ground floor houses a Gap flagship store.

POINTS OF INTEREST

Hyatt Regency 5 Embarcadero Center, 415-788-1234

Palace Hotel (Pied Piper Bar) 2 New Montgomery St., 415-512-1111

House of Shields 39 New Montgomery St., 415-392-7732

route summary

1. Begin at Justin Herman Plaza, at the foot of Market St.
2. Head up one block, west to Drumm St., and hook right into the Hyatt Regency.
3. Come out onto Market St., cross, and head west to New Montgomery; turn left, walk half a block to enter Palace Hotel.
4. Inside Palace hotel, walk to Garden Court, then follow hall back to Market St.
5. Continue on Market to Powell St.

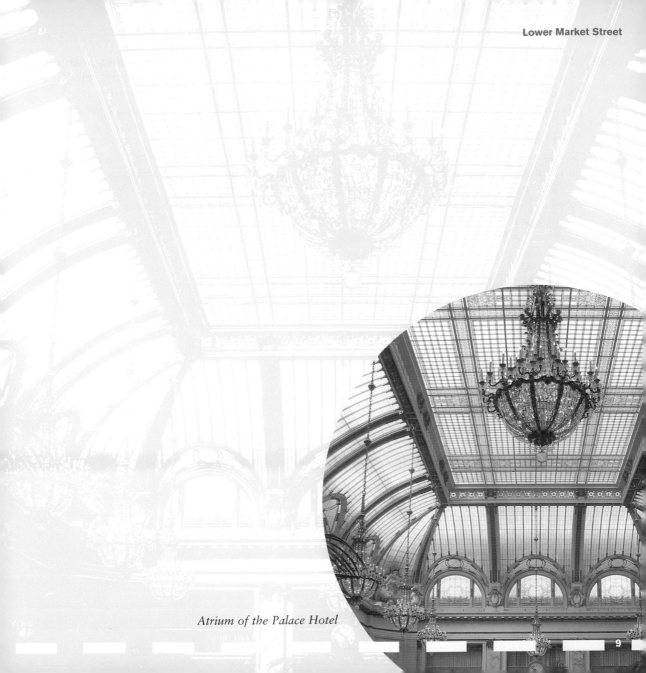

Atrium of the Palace Hotel

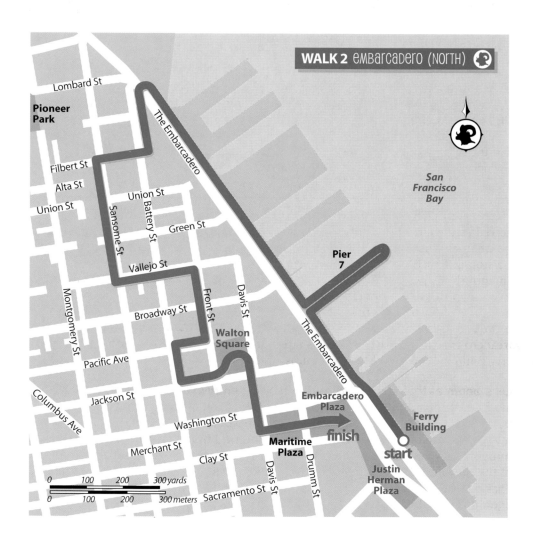

San Francisco Bay

Lombard St

Pioneer Park

The Embarcadero

Filbert St

Alta St

Union St

Union St

Sansome St

Battery St

Green St

Vallejo St

Montgomery St

Broadway St

Front St

Davis St

Pacific Ave

Walton Square

Jackson St

Columbus Ave

Washington St

Merchant St

Clay St

Maritime Plaza

Davis St

Drumm St

Sacramento St

Pier 7

The Embarcadero

Embarcadero Plaza

finish

start

Ferry Building

Justin Herman Plaza

0   100   200   300 yards
0   100   200   300 meters

2 emBarCaDero (NorTH): CoVeriNG THe waTerFroNT

BOUNDARIES: Market St., Embarcadero, Chestnut St., Sansome St.
DISTANCE: 2¼ miles
DIFFICULTY: Easy
PARKING: There is off-street parking at the Embarcadero Center and on Howard St.
PUBLIC TRANSIT: Embarcadero BART station; F streetcar; Muni underground trains;
14, 71 Muni buses

Much of the history of early San Francisco centered on the waterfront around Yerba Buena Cove, which curved into what is now the Financial District as far inland as Battery St. Most of the ground we'll tread on this tour actually rests on the bones of rotted ships, many of which were abandoned by seamen who made a dash for the diggings in the Sierra foothills. Some deserted ships became boarding houses, while others were converted into saloons. One even served as the city jail. Eventually, their wooden hulls formed the foundation for landfill, and the wharves where they tied up became the city streets we walk today. For the unwary sailor, a stop in Frisco was perilous indeed, with swindlers and crimps seeming friendly enough until the hapless seaman was drugged or slugged and sold to the next ship embarking on a two-year voyage. This practice was prevalent in other ports, but it ran rampant in San Francisco, where it became known as "shanghaiing." We'll uncover some of that history here, so keep your wits about ye. This tour doesn't dwell exclusively on the past, though, for the Embarcadero is returning to life after its late 20th century slumber. Saturday morning, when the Ferry Building Farmers' Market is on, is a good time to explore the neighborhood.

● Let's begin at the Ferry Building, the historic entryway to the city for travelers arriving from the East Bay. Built in 1898, the Ferry Building quickly became one of the busiest transit hubs in the world, with some 100,000 passengers passing through every day. The completion of the Bay Bridge had the natural effect of reducing traffic through the Ferry Building, but the bigger insult came in 1959 with the construction of the elevated Embarcadero Freeway, which obscured the building from Market St. That proved to be a temporary problem, solved by the 1989 earthquake, which damaged the elevated freeway. The freeway was demolished a few years later, giving new life to the Ferry Building. Thus, the landmark has survived the 1906 earthquake, the demise of ferry traffic, the intrusion of a freeway, and the 1989 quake. Its future looks as secure as ever now that the ground floor has been converted into an atmospheric marketplace with shops and eateries specializing in gourmet foods. The Ferry Building Marketplace takes the shopping mall food court concept to a new level, with a tasteful style that appeals to locals and tourists alike. When the farmers' market is on (Tuesday and Saturday 8 a.m.–2 p.m. year-round, Thursday 4 p.m.–8 p.m. in summer, Sunday 8 a.m.–2 p.m. in summer) the Ferry Plaza and Marketplace bustle with vendors and crowds of people delving into San Francisco's passionate culture of food. Ferries continue to launch here, too. Walk through the building and around it, past the benches offering front-row views of the bay, Treasure Island, the Bay Bridge, and the Port of Oakland beyond. The fine Slanted Door, a Vietnamese restaurant, anchors the dining scene here.

● Exit the front of the Ferry Building and turn right onto the Embarcadero, which has also been dubbed Herb Caen Way to commemorate the legendary columnist for the San Francisco *Chronicle* and *Examiner*. Caen, who was fond of calling the city "Baghdad by the Bay," would be sad to know of the current condition of the Iraqi capital, but relieved to know that San Francisco hasn't suffered a similar fate. Caen wrote his elliptical gossip column for some 60 years, until his death in February 1997.

● Just past Pier 3, near the foot of Broadway, is the Pier 7 pedestrian wharf, which extends 900 feet out into the bay. Walk out and you're likely to encounter men and women casting their lines. The pier, built in 1990, juts out into the bay in roughly the spot where ships docked at the old Broadway Pier. Piers extended out from Vallejo and Pacific streets as well. Running perpendicular to these piers, Front St. stood on wooden pilings driven into the mud of the bay as late as the mid-1860s. Boardinghouses and saloons crowded around the wharves in a town still short on housing and women. You'll need to use your imagination to picture any of this today.

● At Pier 15, you're likely to spot a few tractor tugs operated by Baydelta Maritime. On the sidewalk here, look for a historical marker entitled "Barbary Coast," which has some tasty excerpts from author Herbert Asbury and historian H.H. Bancroft, describing the rough and tumble entertainment district that was centered along Pacific Ave. just west of here.

- A little ways down the Embarcadero, the Pier 23 Cafe is your basic, squat wooden shack on the wharf, with seafood, a bar, and live music most nights. Sunday afternoon (live jazz from 4 p.m. to 8 p.m.) is also a popular time to drop by, especially when the weather is agreeable and you can relax on the back patio overlooking the bay. Just beyond the restaurant, Pier 23 itself still functions as a warehouse for goods shipped in from overseas. If the gates are open, you'll spot pallets loaded up with imported goods, mostly from the PRC.

- Cross the Embarcadero at Lombard or Chestnut St., and have a look at the Fog City Diner, a spangly reinterpretation of the traditional East Coast diner. The food here is also a reinterpretation, with the kitchen applying some of the principles of California Cuisine to classic fare served up in diners and seafood grills.

- Follow Battery St. a few paces past the Fog City Diner and detour into the small public space behind it, following the path through the little stream and fountain. This is an extension of Levi Strauss Plaza, corporate headquarters for the company that put blue jeans on the legs of the world. German–born Levi Strauss arrived in San Francisco in 1853 and came up with the idea to make durable canvas pants for miners. The campus-like office complex, built in the early 1980s, incorporates modern structures along with a pair of stately warehouses dating to the early 1900s. Cut through the central quad on your way to Sansome St. and turn left.

- Two blocks down, in the nondescript industrial structure at 200 Green St., Philo T. Farnsworth invented television. Farnsworth, a native of Utah, publicly demonstrated his invention for the first time in 1927. He lived until 1971, long

Ferry Building

enough to have watched broadcasts of *Mr. Ed,* the *Beverly Hillbillies,* and the landing of Apollo 11 on the moon.

- The corner of Sansome and Green was also the northeastern extent of a neighborhood known during the Gold Rush as Sydney Town, largely inhabited by ex-cons from Australia. The inhabitants of this menacing little fun-zone, which extended west to Kearny and south to Broadway, were known as the Sydney Ducks, and by and large were considered to be ruffians or worse by the town's few law-abiding citizens.

- At Vallejo St. turn left and continue to Front St. The building on the corner, at 855 Front St., is the Daniel Gibb warehouse, built in 1855. It's a rare Gold-Rush-era survivor that would have originally been located on landfill, at the shore of the bay. Gibb was an importer of goods ranging from liquor to coal. It now is an office building, but looks much as it would have 150 years ago.

- Follow Front St. down to Pacific Ave. and turn right. At Battery, the Old Ship Saloon is a lovely old bar with a dark past. This establishment has an indelible link to James Laflin, one of the city's most notorious shanghaiers. The building dates to 1907, but stands where the business has stood since 1849. The establishment was originally in an old ship, the *Arkansas,* which was abandoned by a crew excited by news of gold strikes. The *Arkansas* docked here and her forecastle was transformed into a drinking tavern before the spot was converted to landfill. Laflin sailed over on the *Arkansas* as a cabin boy and became a bartender in the Old Ship Saloon. He soon gained infamy as one of the city's most successful crimps, selling unconscious seamen to ships sailing out in the morning. A model of the *Arkansas* hangs over the street corner, above the bar's main entrance. Have a drink here—you probably won't end up in Shanghai.

- Turn left onto Battery, then left again at Jackson. Enter the old portals to Sydney Walton Square, now an open space but once the sight of numerous saloons, including the Boston House, run by James "Shanghai" Kelly, whose legend circled the globe. The location of his saloon would have been the corner of Pacific and Davis streets. Pass through the square, admiring the public art and the fountain, and continue through Ferry Park to the Embarcadero.

BACK STORY: SHANGHAIING

Among San Francisco's gifts to the English language is "shanghai," the verb. Sailors put aboard ships against their will were said to have been "shanghaied" by crimps who made a good living through such dastardly deeds. Bill Pickelhaupt, in his book *Shanghaied in San Francisco*, nicely explains the term's etymology. According to Pickelhaupt, during the mid-19th century, Shanghai, China, was not on direct shipping routes from San Francisco, so a sea voyage to that port necessarily involved an indirect course around the globe that took about two years before a sailor returned to San Francisco. Sailors almost always had to be persuaded, honestly or otherwise, to accept such assignments. In San Francisco, a perpetual shortage of seamen—often due to the opportunities and distractions available in the boisterous boomtown—led to an increase in crimping. Crimps sold unconscious sailors to shipping companies in return for the sailors' first two months' wages. Most often the destination was not actually Shanghai. Though the practice was illegal, politicians and businessmen saw the value in looking the other way. Crimps with names like "Shanghai" Kelly and "Shanghai Chicken" Devine obviously felt no need to hide the nature of their business. Kelly's knockout cocktail, served in his saloon, was a mixture of schnapps, beer, and a narcotic—usually opium.

POINTS OF INTEREST

Slanted Door 1 Ferry Building, 415-861-8032

Pier 23 Cafe Pier 23, 415-362-5125

Fog City Diner 1300 Battery St., 415-982-2000

Old Ship Saloon 298 Pacific Ave., 415-788-2222

route summary

1. Begin at the Ferry Building, at the foot of Market St.

2. Exiting the Ferry Building, turn right onto the Embarcadero, heading north.

3. Walk along the Embarcadero, past Pier 23, cross the Embarcadero at Lombard St. or Chestnut St. and return down the other side, heading south.

4. Where Battery St. begins, follow it on the left side of the street for less than a block and turn into the park.

5. Follow the trail through the park until it reaches Levi Plaza.

6. Turn right, into the Plaza, and follow the open quad to Sansome St.

7. Turn left onto Sansome St.

8. Turn left on Vallejo St.

9. Turn right on Front St.

10. Turn right on Pacific St.

11. Turn left on Battery St.

12. Turn left on Jackson St.

13. Turn left on Front St.

14. Enter Sydney Walton Place, cut through the park toward the exit at the corner of Davis and Jackson streets.

15. Cut through Ferry Park, follow trail back to the Embarcadero.

Sailor's delight—the Old Ship Saloon

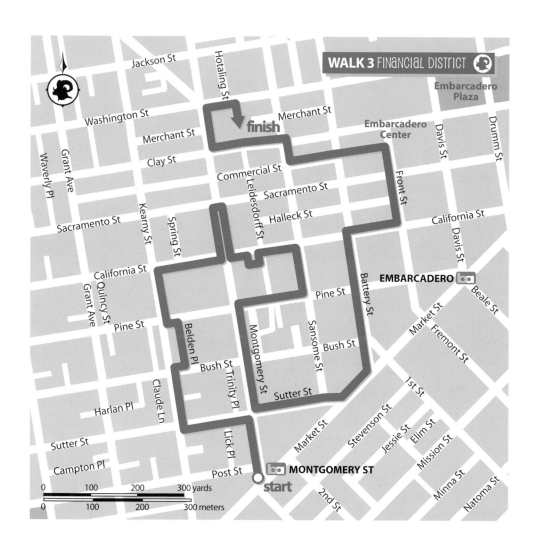

WALK 3 FINANCIAL DISTRICT

Jackson St

Hotaling St

Embarcadero Plaza

Washington St

Merchant St

finish

Merchant St

Embarcadero Center

Davis St

Drumm St

Merchant St

Clay St

Grant Ave

Waverly Pl

Commercial St

Sacramento St

Leidesdorff St

Front St

California St

Sacramento St

Halleck St

Davis St

Kearny St

Spring St

California St

Quincy St

Grant Ave

Pine St

EMBARCADERO

Pine St

Battery St

Beale St

Belden Pl

Bush St

Trinity Pl

Montgomery St

Sansome St

Bush St

Market St

Fremont St

Harlan Pl

Claude Ln

Sutter St

1st St

Sutter St

Lick Pl

Market St

Stevenson St

Jessie St

Elim St

Mission St

Campton Pl

Post St

MONTGOMERY ST

start

2nd St

Minna St

Natoma St

0   100   200   300 yards

0   100   200   300 meters

3 FINANCIAL DISTRICT: THROUGH THE PILLARS OF CAPITALISM

BOUNDARIES: **Market St., Kearny St., Washington St., Front St.**
DISTANCE: **1¾ miles**
DIFFICULTY: **Easy**
PARKING: **none**
PUBLIC TRANSIT: **Montgomery St. BART; Muni underground station; Market St. buses.**

This is where the big wheels turn in San Francisco. Looking much like a section of Manhattan or the Loop in Chicago, the Financial District is a grid of canyons formed by the high-rise pillars of capitalism. Buildings bold, stately, and conservative tell the secret that lies at the core of San Francisco's history and character; for while the cultural icons of the city are gold diggers, gays, and hippies, it was the staunch businesses of banking, stock brokering, real estate, and shipping that put the city on the map. The Financial District, in fact, largely resulted from a real estate scramble, for when San Francisco was founded much of this area was underwater. During the Gold Rush, each time valuable bayfront lots were sold, a little more bay was filled, creating new bayfront property. (It was tough luck for the guy with last year's dockside office.) It's not particularly comforting to consider that skyscrapers and landfill make an unhealthy combination in earthquake country. San Francisco's skyline remained relatively low until quake-resistant steel-frame construction came into vogue. The foundations of the district's skyscrapers stand on pilings driven deep into the earth, and the more modern towers are designed to sway gently in a temblor. The Financial District may be cold at heart, but during workdays its sidewalks are alive with fast-paced, cell-phone-driven human activity. Restaurants, small museums, and rooftop observatories afford the interloper ample opportunity to see the district from the inside out.

● **Start at the former Crocker Bank Building, now owned by Wells Fargo, at 1 Montgomery St. The fine columned entry makes an effective statement on this prominent corner, but what's really interesting about the building is that it was once ten stories taller. It was truncated in the mid-1960s to broaden the views from the Wells Fargo tower behind it. The lowered roof is an open observatory, so go inside, take the elevator up, and have a look around.**

- Follow Montgomery to Sutter and turn left. Half a block up, at No. 130, is the Halladie Building, noted for being among the first glass-curtain-wall buildings in the world. It is a glass face hung on a steel frame—not at all rare today, but unique in 1917 when it was built. Willis Polk designed it. Note the curved fire escapes, designed to enhance the building's looks as well as provide a way out in the event of a blaze.

- At Kearny turn right, cross at Bush St. and turn right again. At the corner of Belden Place and Bush, Sam's Grill is a neighborhood institution with a traditional San Francisco menu based on seafood, pasta, and sourdough bread. The interior booths have curtains, for the privacy of patrons who need to hash out a shady deal. It's not romantic, but very cool in its Sam Spade urbanness.

- Head up Belden, a one-block pedestrian alley that's lined with French restaurants. The area, including Bush St., is known as the "French Ghetto." During the lunch and dinner hours, especially on warm days, the alley is crammed with little tables where off-duty white collar workers enjoy mussels from Plouf or steak frites from Cafe Bastille.

- At the end of Belden Place, hook left and continue down Kearny, walking in the shadow of the Bank of America Building, which stands 52 stories tall. It was San Francisco's tallest building until the Transamerica Pyramid went up a few years later. Look up from any perspective, and the building's striking, sawtooth bays, slicing into the sky, catch and reflect light and color. In front of the building, wide steps meet a raised plaza with a hulking black sculpture that's informally known as the "Banker's Heart." You can ride elevators to the top floor, but the only way to enjoy a view is over an overpriced drink in the Carnelian Room.

- Follow Kearny to Sacramento St., turn right, and turn right again at Montgomery. The Wells Fargo History Museum is worth a quick visit to get a rosy perspective on one of the city's biggest and oldest financial institutions. (Wells Fargo opened its first office in San Francisco in 1852.) Most visitors are lured in for an up-close look at the old stagecoach. In addition to banking, Wells Fargo initially ran a network of stages across the Western U.S. until the arrival of the railroads. Admission is free.

- At the corner of Montgomery and California—the heart of the Financial District—turn right. The Merchants Exchange Building (465 California St.) is a Daniel Burnham design and reflects his Chicago School architectural style. It was built in 1903. Enter the building and pass through the long lobby to enter the California Bank Trust, where the glory of the building's maritime past is celebrated with huge murals by Walter Coulter and Nils Hagerup. Architect Julia Morgan once kept her offices on the top floor of the building.

- Exit a side door onto tiny Leidesdorff St., a narrow lane that appears determined not to attract attention. Before the 1906 quake, Leidesdorff was known as "Pauper Alley." As wild speculation on silver mining went on elsewhere in the district, Leidesdorff was lined with small-time exchanges where the nearly penniless could invest a few cents in hopes of turning their luck around. The street apparently had few, if any, rags-to-riches tales.

- Return to California St., and opposite, on the corner of Sansome, you'll spot the imposing Bank of California, a monumental, mausoleum-like structure erected in 1908. Step inside and you'll see that the entire building is, essentially, one huge, cavernous room with enough airspace beneath its vaulted ceiling to fly a small airplane, if such a thing were permitted. It's a glorious waste of space. Down in the basement, a small museum (free admission) has a few intriguing items, including gold nuggets imbedded in chunks of quartz and some territorial gold coins and shiny ingots from the Gold Rush.

- Turn right at Sansome and right again at Pine. On the opposite corner is the

Wells Fargo Bank

Pacific Stock Exchange. Stockbrokers once worked here, and now that it has become a fitness club they work out here. The building was constructed in 1915, and apparently the stock market crash necessitated a 1930 remodeling job, which added designs by Timothy Pfleuger. The stoic sculpted figures on both sides of the broad front stairway are by Ralph Stackpole, who in the early 20th century was a central figure in the city's art scene. A side entrance on Sansome leads to the private City Club, in which a two-story mural by Diego Rivera graces a stairwell, which can be seen by nonmembers on a guided tour (call 415-648-7198).

● Turn left at Montgomery, onto a block dominated by two handsome landmarks. The Russ Building, at No. 235, was the city's tallest for several decades after it was built in 1928. Opposite, at No. 220, the Mills Building is the city's archetypal Chicago-style office building. A Daniel Burnham–John Wellborn Root collaboration, it was built in 1892 and survived the 1906 catastrophe, though extensive remodeling was required. It was the first all-steel-frame structure in the city.

● At Sutter St. turn left. At the corner of Sutter and Sansome is the Citicorp Center, which was built in 1910 and

BACK STORY: FRANK CHU

While walking along Montgomery St., you might run into Frank Chu, a man who always has something on his mind and puts it on a sign, which he carries up and down the street nearly every day. He's been walking this beat, sharing his cryptic views, since 1996. For years, Chu advocated impeaching President Bill Clinton, even after Clinton was no longer president. Locals have taken an interest in this eccentric character, mostly because the Frank Chu message turns out to be as bizarre and intricately worked out as you might imagine. Many of Chu's signs refer to the "12 Galaxies," which he claims influenced Clinton to commit treason. He also holds Clinton responsible for not paying Chu for appearing in a reality TV show called "The Richest Family." Adidas and Quiznos have paid to put advertising on his signs, and the 12 Galaxies nightclub in the Mission District, whose name was inspired by Chu, lets him drink at the bar for free. Amid the wage slaves and desk jockeys of the Financial District, Frank Chu stands out as an individual who has found a unique way to make a living.

gutted in 1984, reducing it to an atrium for a new adjacent tower. Beyond the cafe tables and fountain, you'll spot the "Star Girl" statue. She's a sight for sore eyes, a replica of a parapet ornament from the Panama Pacific Exposition, which took place in the Marina District in 1914.

● Turn left onto Market St., and to your left is the green-tinted Crown Zellerbach Building, a glass-curtain beauty from 1959. Unlike nearly every other building in the cramped Financial District, the Crown Zellerbach is set off the street, with paved grounds surrounding it.

● Turn left at Battery and left again at Bush, where two contrasting structures stand side by side. The elegant Shell Building, at 100 Bush, is a sleek skyscraper clad in terra-cotta. It dwarfs its neighbor, the pencil-thin Heineman Building, at No. 130. Built in 1910, it makes the fullest use of its narrow, 20-foot lot.

● Loop around to California St. via Sansome, Pine, and Battery. At 240 California St., half a block off Battery, Tadich Grill is a revered establishment. It can claim to be the oldest restaurant in the city, having opened in 1849. It has occupied its present site since the late 1960s, and it has the atmosphere of a much older place because the older location (on Clay St.) was stripped, moved, and reassembled here. Busy as ever, Tadich continues to please diners hankering for Frisco traditions such as sand dabs, seafood cioppino, and Anchor Steam beer.

● At Front St. turn left and head into the Embarcadero Center. This four-tower complex, with a shopping center on the bottom two floors and offices above, was loosely modeled on New York's Rockefeller Center. Walk up the winding stairs to the second level, and follow the footbridge that crosses over Battery St. As you cross you'll get a good vantage of the Old Federal Reserve Building, an imposing neo-Classical structure built in 1924. You can walk right through the lobby, which is graced by a Jules Guerin mural.

● Come down a ramp to Sansome St., turn right, and proceed to Clay St. Follow Clay St. to Montgomery and the Transamerica Building, which for obvious reasons is commonly known as the Transamerica Pyramid. Standing 853 feet, it is the tallest building in San Francisco. Initially after it was completed in 1972 it was unpopular, mostly for being so conspicuous. Some detractors needled architect William Pereira by calling it "Pereira's Prick." By now, it is difficult to imagine San Francisco's skyline without the pyramid's pointed top. Walk around the building, and on the Washington St. side you'll find an entrance to Redwood Park, a fine spot to end this tour, amidst the tallest trees and the tallest building.

POINTS OF INTEREST

Sam's Grill 374 Bush St., 415-421-0594

Plouf 40 Belden Place, 415-986-6491

Café Bastille 22 Belden Place, 415-986-5673

Wells Fargo History Museum 420 Montgomery St., 415-396-2619

City Club 155 Sansome St., 415-648-7198

Tadich Grill 240 California St., 415-391-1849

ROUTE SUMMARY

1. Start at the corner of Montgomery and Market streets and head north, into the Financial District.
2. Turn left at Sutter St.
3. Turn right at Kearny St.
4. Cross Bush St., turn right, and then left onto Belden Place.
5. Go back, then turn left on Pine St.
6. Make an immediate right on Kearny; continue to Sacramento St. and turn right.
7. Turn right at Montgomery St.
8. Turn left at California St.
9. Make a brief detour to Leidesdorff St.
10. Turn right at Sansome St.
11. Turn right at Pine St.
12. Turn left at Montgomery St.
13. Turn left at Sutter St.
14. Head left (east) on Market St.

15. Turn left at Battery St.
16. Turn left at Bush St.
17. Turn right at Sansome St.
18. Turn right at Pine St.
19. Turn left at Battery St.
20. Turn right at California.
21. Turn left at Front St.
22. At the Embarcadero, turn left to go up winding stairs beneath the pedestrian overpass.
23. On the second level cross the pedestrian overpass, follow it past Battery St. and down a ramp.
24. Turn right at Sansome St.
25. Turn left at Clay St.
26. Turn right at Montgomery St.
27. Turn right at Washington St. and go to the Transamerica Building.
28. Enter Redwood Park.

Federal Reserve Building

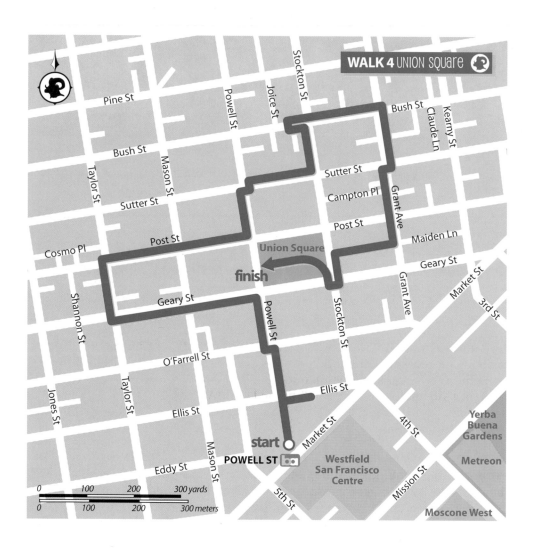

Pine St

Stockton St

Powell St

Joice St

Bush St

Kearny St

Claude Ln

Bush St

Taylor St

Mason St

Sutter St

Sutter St

Campton Pl

Grant Ave

Post St

Post St

Cosmo Pl

Maiden Ln

Union Square

Geary St

finish

Shannon St

Geary St

Stockton St

Grant Ave

Market St

3rd St

Powell St

O'Farrell St

Taylor St

Ellis St

4th St

Ellis St

Jones St

Yerba Buena Gardens

Metreon

start

Market St

Mason St

POWELL ST

Westfield San Francisco Centre

Mission St

Eddy St

5th St

Moscone West

0   100   200   300 yards

0   100   200   300 meters

4 UNION SQUARE: MINING THE COMMERCIAL MOTHER LODE

BOUNDARIES: **Market St., Taylor St., Bush St., Grant Ave.**
DISTANCE: **1½ miles**
DIFFICULTY: **Moderately Easy (one hill, some stairs)**
PARKING: **Off-street parking is available at the 5th and Mission Garage, a block south of the start of this tour.**
PUBLIC TRANSIT: **Powell St. BART station; underground Muni light rail, streetcars, and Market St. buses all stop at the starting point for this tour. So do Powell St. cable cars.**

With its historic buildings, showpiece retail stores, fine restaurants, theaters, hotels, billboards clamoring for rooftop exposure, and converging public transit lines, Union Square has all the hallmarks of a commercial and cultural hub. It's a central crossroads that has a way of drawing people and traffic through it. Day and night, the area buzzes with autos, footfalls, the groaning of cable car brakes, street corner singers, and the toot of whistles blown by hotel doormen hailing cabs. This tour will range a bit freely, meandering from Market St. to Union Square itself in the least direct route possible.

● Start at the Powell St. cable car turnaround, on the corner of Market and Powell. If it's spring or summer, a hundred or more people will be lined up here for a ride on the historic cable cars, and a multitude of street performers will be vying for their attention (and spare change). Don't get in line, but wait for a cable car to come along, and watch how it is rolled onto the circular platform, then rotated 180 degrees, all by hand just as it has been done for over 130 years.

● Overlooking the cable car turnaround is the staunch and impressive Flood Building, now home to a huge Gap flagship store occupying the ground floor. The building is a quake survivor. It was designed by Albert Pissis and built in 1904. Dashiell Hammett worked upstairs for the Pinkerton Agency during the early 1920s, a few years before he published the novels that would make him a famous crime-fiction writer. Walk along Powell St., around the block-long Flood Building, and hook right on Ellis St. Half a block up you'll spot John's Grill, which has been operating since 1908.

Hammett reputedly dined at John's frequently, and even mentioned the place in his best novel, *The Maltese Falcon.*

● Return to Powell and turn right. The street is a disorganized mélange of shops geared to tourists and passers-through. In the mix are some age-old establishments that seem to hang on despite the changing vibe of the neighborhood. These blocks of Powell St. not so long ago had some of the Tenderloin's flophouse atmosphere. Tad's Steaks, with its excellent, gaudy sign looking like a holdover from the vaudeville era, still serves shoe-leather cuts, charbroiled and served over the counter. At Powell and O'Farrell, Marquard's Little Cigar Store closed a few years back but its great curved sign, wrapping around the corner, remains. Some San Franciscans lamented the closing of the shop, but it turns out they really only thought they'd miss the sign. Near the corner of Geary, the Gold Spike keeps alcoholic hours (opening at 6 a.m.), and boasts a nightly lineup of Dixieland jazz. San Francisco was way into Dixieland long after New York went bop and L.A. went cool. The Gold Spike just goes on being a friendly little joint that doesn't give a damn what year it is.

● Turn left on Geary, and more roughs appear amidst the diamonds. Lefty O'Doul's is named for a nearly forgotten baseball hero who won the National League batting crown in 1929, finishing just two points shy of a .400 average. He led the league again three seasons later. The bar's a great spot for perusing local sports memorabilia, and the stools have baseball bats for legs. It's also a bustling hofbrau where the hot open-faced turkey sandwich is a fine mess to get yourself into. At night someone tinkles the ivories and others sing along.

● At the corner of Geary and Mason stands the Pinecrest Diner, a 24-hour eatery that's been slinging the neighborhood's hash since 1969. Looks like it's been here longer than that. The food won't compete with Mom's, unless Mom operates her own greasy spoon. It's the no-nonsense, Hopper-painting atmosphere that draws people. The place is genuinely hard-boiled, and a little tragic. In 1997, a grill cook shot and killed a waitress in the restaurant. Look for her photo on the wall behind the counter.

● The Pinecrest inadvertently ushers us into the Theater District, where two landmark stages stand side by side on the block. The Geary Theater opened in 1909 and is now home of the highly respected American Conservatory Theater. The building is a beauty clad in terra-cotta tiles, many of them shaped like fruit. It's best admired from across the street. Next door, the Curran was built in 1922, and though it's not bearing fruit, it and the Geary make a very compatible pair. Theaters small and large are scattered all throughout the neighborhood.

- At the end of the block stands the Clift Hotel, which through a recent remodel has successfully entered the ranks of the city's most sophisticated hostelries. The Clift always had the Redwood Room, a gorgeous, clubby old watering hole, and those in the know long appreciated their martinis here. The joint's fashionable now, with a velvet rope and a bouncer. If things ever cool off it will once again be relaxed place for having a drink amidst early 20th century splendor.

- Across from the Clift is another pompous old hotel, the Monaco, which has retained much of its steamship-era pizazz. You need only step into the hotel's restaurant, the Grand Cafe, to get an idea of how much pampering goes on here. In a former ballroom, the Grand makes a convincing argument that size matters. There's plenty of room for left-handers at the tables here, and it probably takes two lefties to change the light bulbs—one to screw in the bulb, one to hold the ladder. It's a good spot for lunch, if eating is in your plans.

- Turn right at Taylor St. Halfway up the block look for tiny Isadora Duncan Lane, a model for how all dead-end alleys ought to look. It's named for the legendary dancer, who was born within a block of here. At the corner of Post is another great old bar, C. Bobby's Owl Tree, noted principally for its single-minded obsession with owl-themed art. The collection was assembled by Bobby Cook, who owned and ran the place for 30 years,

The Flood Building

until his untimely death in 2006. Owl paintings, owl figurines, owl clocks, and even a few stuffed specimens hang from the ceiling, cover the walls, and fill display cases. The chairs swivel so you can spin around and take it all in. Despite its eccentricities, C. Bobby's has the dignified air of an old man in a hat and tie, much as the late Bobby C did.

● The Bohemian Club stands kitty-corner from the Owl Tree in a stately, ivy-covered, red-brick fortress. The owl is a Bohemian Club symbol, but supposedly this is merely a coincidence. The name was once somewhat appropriate, for when it was founded, in 1872, the club's members were writers, poets, newspaper reporters, and artists. By 1900, however, the club was dominated by businessmen and social elites. All men, of course, and all white. The club hasn't changed much (it's now about 2 percent non-white). U.S. presidents have attended the club's annual summer fetes, held two hours north of the city in the Bohemian Grove. George W. Bush and Dick Cheney had a powwow at the Grove in 2000, which supposedly resulted in Cheney joining the Republican ticket. A plaque on the side of the club has a bas-relief owl on a branch, along with the words "Weaving spiders come not here"—meaning what? No knitting widows allowed? The vast majority of San Franciscans live happily beyond the pale and regard the Bohemian Club with distrust and disdain.

● Turn right on Post St. and cross Mason St. On the south side of the street is Postrio, owned by celebrity chef Wolfgang Puck and lauded for its California Cuisine. On the north side of the street is Farallon, one of the city's best seafood restaurants. Step inside for a look at the outlandish decor, which includes illuminated jellyfish hanging from the ceiling.

● At Powell turn left. Two local landmarks face off on this block. On the west side is humble Sears' Fine Foods, known the world over for its dollar-sized pancakes. It was opened in 1938 by Ben Sears. Nearly every reference to Sears mentions he was a retired circus clown, so let's not overlook that important detail. Opposite is the Drake Hotel. Cross at Sutter and backtrack to the hotel's front entrance and be sure to smile at the Beefeater doorman on your way in. Inside, examine the magnificent staircase with its intricate cast-iron rail, and gape at the molded plaster ceiling above. Then duck downstairs, where an elevator can take you to the Starlight Room, a swanky top-floor nightclub surrounded by plate-glass windows. Back at the bottom floor, leave the Drake through the side exit, onto Sutter St.; cross at the light and turn right.

- The office tower at 450 Sutter is mostly populated by doctors and dentists, but the building is a pure flight of fancy. The lobby looks like a Cecil B. DeMille set—an Aztecan temple, say. Worth going in for a look-see. The tower's jagged columns of bay windows are fine to look at too.

- At Stockton St. turn left, and you're soon facing the southern end of the Stockton Tunnel. The entry looks inviting, despite the sign that says "quiet in tunnel," but it's just your usual tunnel, dank and dimly lit. Immediately within, a foul-smelling flight of steps leads up to Bush St., which is where we're headed.

- The Tunnel Top Bar, a refurbished old dive that's kind of hip now, welcomes you to Bush St. Just past it, on a wall flanking narrow Burritt Alley, a plaque notes that Sam Spade's partner, Miles Archer, was "done in" on this spot by Brigid O'Shaughnessy. It's great to see completely fictional events getting historic markers. You can walk away with this lesson: always cross-check anything you've read on a plaque. On the other side of the street, another alley is named for Hammett.

- Now turn around and walk down Bush. Elegant Notre Dame des Victoires, a French Catholic church, stands at No. 564. It was originally built in 1855, then rebuilt after the '06 quake. The organ, which was installed in 1915, is a beauty.

- At Grant turn right, stopping for a quick look at the groovy Hotel Triton, a boutique hostelry that trades on the city's countercultural heritage. For the heck of it ask to see a room and you might be shown the Carlos Santana or Jerry Garcia suites (supposedly with design input from these guys) or a tiny "Zen den."

- The southeast corner of Grant and Sutter streets is dominated by the historic White House department store, which closed its doors years ago. The building is now occupied by Banana Republic. It was designed, with Federalist overtones, by Albert Pissis, and built in 1908.

- Turn right onto slender Maiden Lane, a street that had its name changed in order to obscure a shameful past. Before the '06 quake the street, then known as Morton St., was known as one of the city's dreariest hubs of prostitution. Low-life cribs lined both sides of the street. It's much calmer and more respectable now. All there is to see is the Xanadu Gallery, a store that sells fine artifacts and folk art from exotic, far-off lands. The building is a Frank Lloyd Wright design built in 1949, and its spiral ramp is often cited as a "warm-up" act for Wright's more accomplished Guggenheim Museum in New York.

- Maiden Lane ends at Union Square. Turn left, walk to the corner of Geary and enter the Neiman Marcus department store. Immediately within, stare up at the great rotunda, with its stained-glass mosaic of a ship. It's all that remains of the old City of Paris department store that formerly stood on this corner. The rest of the building was demolished and replaced by the current modern structure in the early 1980s. You can take an elevator to the top floor for a closer look at the glass, or get back out now before someone sprays perfume on you.

- Cross to the square. It was part of the original city plans of 1850, and became a more prominent address as the city expanded south from Portsmouth Square. It gained its name during the Civil War. The Dewey Monument, rising like a pin from the square's center, commemorates a victory in the Spanish American War. A parking structure—meant to double as a bomb shelter—was dug beneath the square during World War II. The square acquired its current Italian piazza styling in a dot-com-era overhaul. It's a good spot to stop for an outdoor coffee or to see occasional midday music performances. The surrounding cityscape of department stores, billboards, and the awesome St. Francis Hotel makes this a pleasant urban space. You're seeing the St. Francis from its most flattering vantage point. Head in the hotel's direction and we'll conclude our tour in its lobby.

- The St. Francis was built in 1904, and two years later it was gutted by the fires of '06 and rebuilt. It's the grand dame of Union Square, but it hasn't escaped controversy over the years. In 1921 comic actor Fatty Arbuckle rented a suite of rooms here and threw the party that ended with the gruesome death of a young actress, Virginia Rappe. Arbuckle was tried for rape and murder, but he wasn't convicted. The scandal nevertheless diminished his comic appeal and put an end to his career. President

Gerald Ford was shot at by Sarah Jane Moore in front of the hotel in 1975. (She missed.) A modern high-rise annex was built in the early 1970s, with high-speed glass elevators shooting skyward along the east side of the building. For kicks, end the tour with a ride up to the top, and you'll enjoy a spectacular view as well as the sensation of leaving your stomach two or three floors beneath you.

POINTS OF INTEREST

Tad's Steaks 120 Powell St., 415-982-1718

Gold Dust Lounge 247 Powell St., 415-397-1695

Lefty O'Doul's 333 Geary St., 415-982-8900

Pine Crest Diner 401 Geary St., 415-885-6407

Grand Cafe 501 Geary St., 415-292-0101

C. Bobby's Owl Tree 601 Post St., 415-776-9344

Postrio 545 Post St., 415-776-7825

Farallon 450 Post St., 415-956-6969

Sears' Fine Foods 439 Powell St., 415-986-0700

Starlight Room 450 Powell St., 415-395-8595

Tunnel Top 601 Bush St., 415-986-8900

route summary

1. Start at the corner of Powell and Market streets and head up Powell.
2. Turn right on Ellis St., walk half a block up, then return to Powell.
3. Turn right on Powell St.
4. Turn left on Geary St.
5. Turn right on Taylor St.
6. Turn right on Post St.
7. Turn left on Powell St.
8. Turn right on Sutter St.
9. Turn left on Stockton St.
10. At the entrance to the Stockton Tunnel, walk up the stairs to Bush St.
11. Head west on Bush St., half a block. to Burritt Alley.
12. Turn around and head east on Bush St.
13. Turn right on Grant Ave.
14. Turn right on Maiden Lane.
15. Turn left on Stockton St.
16. Cross to Union Square.
17. Cross to the Hotel St. Francis.

The St. Francis Hotel as seen from Union Square

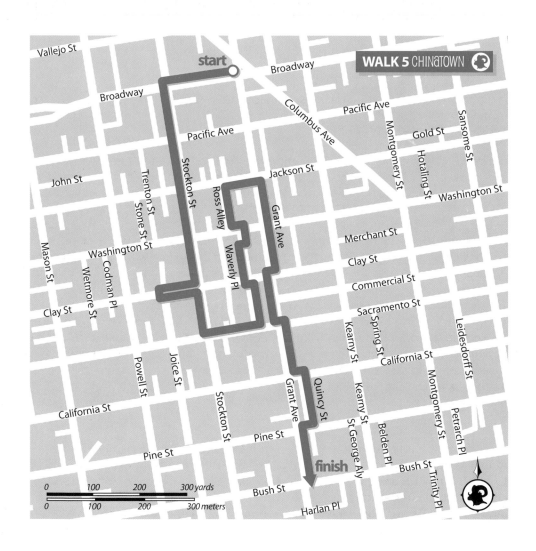

WALK 5 CHINaTOWN

start

Vallejo St

Broadway

Broadway

Columbus Ave

Pacific Ave

Pacific Ave

Montgomery St

Gold St

Hotaling St

Sansome St

Jackson St

Washington St

John St

Trenton St

Stockton St

Ross Alley

Stone St

Waverly Pl

Grant Ave

Merchant St

Clay St

Commercial St

Mason St

Washington St

Codman Pl

Wetmore St

Sacramento St

Spring St

Kearny St

California St

Leidesdorff St

Clay St

Powell St

Joice St

Stockton St

Grant Ave

Quincy St

Kearny St

St George Aly

Belden Pl

Montgomery St

Petrarch Pl

California St

Pine St

Pine St

finish

Bush St

Trinity Pl

Bush St

Pine St

Harlan Pl

0   100   200   300 yards

0   100   200   300 meters

5 CHINATOWN: THE FAR EAST OF THE WEST COAST

BOUNDARIES: **Broadway, Stockton St., Bush St., Grant Ave.**
DISTANCE: **1 ¾ miles**
DIFFICULTY: **Moderately Easy (mild hills)**
PARKING: **Off-street parking is available on Vallejo St., between Powell and Stockton (one block from the starting point for this tour).**
PUBLIC TRANSIT: **30 and 45 Muni buses**

San Francisco has a Chinatown to rival any city's Chinatown, in part due to its outrageous architecture, but mostly because it has all the hustle and bustle you'd expect to find on the streets of Hong Kong. Chinatown was deliberately designed to reflect a naive American idea of Chinese architecture, with buildings that look like pagodas painted in spectacular, often garish colors. Even the lamp posts, fire hydrants, and telephone booths have a kitschy, orientalist look to them. But comparisons to Disneyland really are not fair. In the wake of the '06 quake, men of overwhelming influence, including former mayor James Phelan, wanted to move Chinatown to remote Hunters Point. Chinese businessmen preempted that campaign by rebuilding quickly with over-the-top, undeniably Chinese styles of architecture. Thanks to their efforts, Chinatown stayed put, and to this day it remains one of San Francisco's most vibrant and exciting neighborhoods. Its sidewalks are packed shoulder-to-shoulder with locals every day of the year. Displays of produce, seafood, plastic buckets, silk pajamas, cheap toys, and all manner of goods literally spill out of the shops. At night, the district's commercial streets become a relatively subdued and atmospheric constellation of neon. On this walk we'll wander the main stem, Grant Ave., with frequent detours through mysterious alleys smelling of cabbage, and into clamorous dim sum parlours where you'd hardly know you were still in North America.

● A visit to Chinatown should include a stop for dim sum, and since Gold Mountain, at 644 Broadway, is the quintessential dim sum restaurant, it makes a good place to start. Show up around 11 a.m. and you'll find yourself in a crowded hall alive with chatter, mostly in Cantonese. A fleet of carts rolls through the aisles bearing steaming hot morsels such as silky shrimp crepes, deep-fried shrimp balls, flaky xiu mai, and piping hot pots of congee (rice porridge). Thus fortified, hit the streets and work it off.

● Head up Broadway and turn left onto Stockton St. This is the district's "real," untour-isty side, where the locals shop for everything from produce to hardware. Stroll the next few blocks and duck into the shops that intrigue you. Most of the time the wares are on display out on the sidewalk. Among the tubs of iced-down fish and boxes of freshly picked bok choy you're sure to spot exotic foodstuffs such as armadillos and frogs. Stockton is also the street on which you're most likely to be nudged out of an old lady's way, so watch your step.

● Turn right at Clay St. Half a block up, at No. 965, the Chinese Historical Society of America operates a museum in a former YWCA building. The permanent collection is modest, but special exhibits focusing on Chinese life in California from the Gold Rush to the present are generally worth a look. Admission is $3. The building is no run-of-the-mill gymnasium, having been designed by Julia Morgan.

● Return to Stockton and turn right. The building at No. 843 is home of the Consolidated Benevolent Association, also known as the "Chinese Six Companies." The Six Companies is far more than a family association or social aid club. It is a conglomeration of such community groups that started forming in the late 19th cen-tury, at a time when Chinatown society was continually disrupted by ongoing tong wars between rival criminal gangs. It became for a time the most powerful Chinese American political organization in the country. The Six Companies remains highly influential in San Francisco's Chinese community today.

● Across the street, at No. 836, is Sun Yat-Sen Memorial Hall, and next door to that is the local Kuomintang headquarters. KMT, the Chinese Nationalist Party, vied for control of mainland China from 1912 until the Communist victory in 1949, and then dominated Taiwanese politics for most of the 20th century. It has historically drawn wide support from San Francisco's Chinese community.

● Turn left onto Sacramento St., and at Waverly Place stop in at the Clarion Music Center, a shop that sells beautiful instruments used in the traditional music of China. There's a room devoted to high-quality gongs of all sizes and timbres, and even a full-length lion-dance costume. But the shop's primary emphasis is on the erhu, the two-string spike fiddle played so mournfully in some of the neighborhood's alleys. If you're in a buying mood, rest assured you can also learn to play the instrument here.

- Walk the two-block length of Waverly, a narrow road that's not quite small enough to be considered an alley. In the late 19th century it was lined with barber shops, and because the price of a trim was 15 cents, Waverly was known as "15 Cent Street." There's still a solitary barber shop, near the end of the street, called Ken's, that charges $8.50 for a cut (plus an additional 50 cents if you want a passé "layered" cut, according to the sign out front). Waverly is a colorful street, with many painted balconies and decorative tiles on the facades of the buildings. Signs over the doorways indicate numerous family associations are based here, and there are a smattering of Buddhist temples hidden away on some of the top floors. One, Tin How Temple, is open to visitors (10 a.m. to 4 p.m.). It's well worth the schlep up three flights of stairs for what feels like a privileged behind-the-scenes look in this otherwise private neighborhood. Welcoming volunteers will deliver a prepared narration to explain the altar and the joss sticks spiraling overhead.

- Where Waverly meets Washington, take a quick right to Sam Wo's, where the woeful food is legendary. Years ago, this place was popular simply because its head waiter, who called himself Edsel Ford, was so comically rude to the patrons. Jack Kerouac supposedly learned to use chopsticks here while chomping on chow mein with his friend, the poet Gary Snyder. Sam Wo's is still worth the resulting heartburn for the nonpareil atmosphere—guests pass through the kitchen, up twisting narrow stairs, into cramped unadorned dining rooms, where they are greeted by a mildly rude waiter (following in the late Mr. Ford's footsteps). Meals are shuttled up from the kitchen in a rickety old dumbwaiter.

- Backtrack up Washington, cross the street, and head up Ross Alley, a mysterious passageway known as the

Pagoda-style architecture

"Street of the Gamblers" in the 19th century because so many gambling joints were located here. Down near the end of the block, slip into the Golden Gate Fortune Cookie Company, where you can see how fortune cookies are made. The machinery in the shop looks like it was built in the age of steam engines, and the workers who fold the still-hot cookies, after first slipping the fortunes in, are quick and deft. Someone will stop and sell you a bag of warm cookies if you like, but they're generally too busy to field questions. A couple of doors down, Jun Yu's Barber Shop is easily passed unnoticed, but be sure to pause for a peek inside. It's the world's smallest, most cluttered barbershop, with barely enough room for a chair and a barber to stand in. When business is slow the barber passes the time in front of his shop, reading the paper or bowing his erhu fiddle. You'll notice 4-by-6-inch snaps of celebrities like Matt Dillon and Michael Douglas in the shop window. Over the years the place has attracted the attention of Hollywood location scouts, and a number of films have included scenes shot here. The evidence suggests singer Tom Waits was the only celeb to actually get his ears lowered here.

● At Jackson St. turn right, and at Grant Ave. turn right again. On this block, you'll spot two great old drinking taverns, the garish Li Po (named for a poet) and the more somnolent Buddha Bar (named for a god). Both places look like World War II shore-leave saloons and are good for a quiet cold one.

● Just off Grant at 743 Washington, the Bank of Canton occupies what was once the Chinese Telephone Exchange. The building, constructed after the 1906 quake, is worthy of a movie set. In order to handle the complex mix of cultures and languages in Chinatown, the operators who worked the exchange were fluent in five Chinese dialects in addition to English.

● Return to Grant, and halfway down the block you'll reach the Empress of China, a posh restaurant that had its heyday in the middle of the 20th century. Just enter the lobby (the actual dining room is on the top floor) for a look at the celebrity snaps posted near the elevator. You'll see some comic surprises, including Raymond Burr from his "Ironside" period and a rather exuberant Jayne Mansfield. Loads of others. Have a look.

● Grant Ave. is of course the touristy heart of Chinatown, and it's lined with shops selling kitschy knickknacks. Some are worth picking through. Watch your head on entering the Chinatown Kite Shop, where the impressive stock hangs low from the ceiling. The array of kites is something to behold, with exemplary models shaped like eagles, the *Kitty Hawk,* and a 28-foot-long, multi-section dragon that could have been plucked from the Chinese New Year parade. Nearby, Canton Bazaar has cast-iron teapots, chopsticks, and a selection of "sensual" statues behind a glass case. At least check in to admire the lovely two-story painting hanging in the south stairwell.

● The intersection of Grant and California streets is a pivotal crossroads in Chinatown where you'll find several landmark buildings, including the first two fake pagodas to go up after the '06 quake. The intersection is flanked by the exotic Sing Fat Building, at 717 California St., which went up in 1907, and the Sing Chong Building, at 601 Grant, which went up a year later. Also at this intersection stands Old St. Mary's, a miraculous quake survivor that dates all the way back to 1853. This old church has seen it all, and a sign below the clock quotes Ecclesiastes: "Son, observe the time and fly from evil."

● Cross California, turn left, and make a quick right at Quincy St., into St. Mary's Square. The park is a hidden sanctuary amid the neighborhood's hustle and bustle, and often you'll encounter locals doing their tai chi exercises here. At the center of the square, a statue of Sun Yat-Sen, looking like the tin man in the Wizard of Oz, is the work of sculptor Beniamino Bufano.

● At Pine St., turn right, which gets you back to Grant. Follow it all the way to the Chinatown Gate, at Bush St., and you'll have seen quite a lot of Chinatown. The neighborhood warrants further exploration, so you may want to wander back through all the streets we haven't hit on this tour.

POINTS OF INTEREST

Gold Mountain 644 Broadway, 415-296-7733

The Chinese Historical Society of America 965 Clay St., 415-391-1188

Clarion Music Center 816 Sacramento St., 415-391-1317

Golden Gate Fortune Cookie Company 56 Ross Alley, 415-781-3956

Bank of Canton (Old Chinese Telephone Exchange) 743 Washington St

Chinatown Kite Shop 717 Grant Ave., 415-989-5182

Canton Bazaar 616 Grant Ave., 415-362-5750

route summary

1. Start at Gold Mountain, on Broadway just above Columbus St.
2. Head west on Broadway, then turn left at Stockton St.
3. Turn right at Clay St.
4. Return to Stockton and turn right.
5. Turn left at Sacramento St.
6. Turn left at Waverly Place.
7. Turn right briefly onto Washington St. (for Sam Wo's), then cross and head up Ross Alley.
8. Turn right at Jackson St.
9. Turn right on Grant Ave.
10. Turn right at California St.
11. Turn right at Quincy St., leading into St. Mary's Square.
12. Turn right at Pine St.
13. Turn left at Grant Ave.
14. End at Bush St. at the Chinatown gate.

Sun Yat-Sen, by Beniamino Bufano

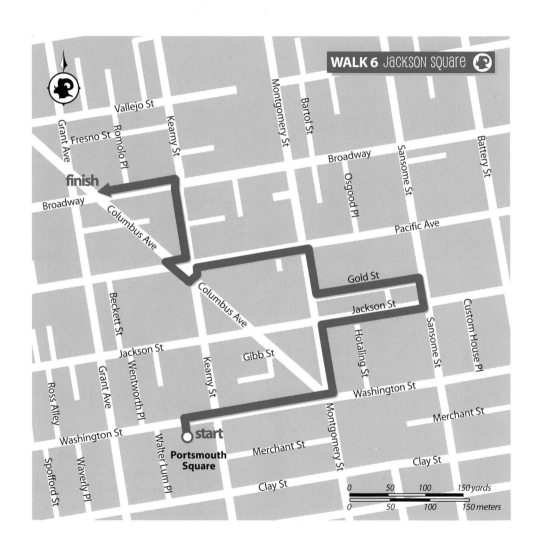

Vallejo St

Grant Ave

Fresno St

Romolo Pl

Kearny St

Montgomery St

Bartol St

Broadway

Sansome St

Battery St

finish

Broadway

Columbus Ave

Osgood Pl

Pacific Ave

Columbus Ave

Gold St

Jackson St

Beckett St

Sansome St

Custom House Pl

Jackson St

Wentworth Pl

Kearny St

Gibb St

Hotaling St

Ross Alley

Grant Ave

Washington St

Washington St

Merchant St

start

Spofford St

Waverly Pl

Walter Lum Pl

Portsmouth Square

Merchant St

Montgomery St

Clay St

Clay St

Clay St

| 0 | 50 | 100 | 150 yards |
| 0 | 50 | 100 | 150 meters |

6 Jackson Square: Time Traveling Through the Barbary Coast

BOUNDARIES: **Washington St., Kearny St., Sansome St., Broadway**
DISTANCE: **¾ mile**
DIFFICULTY: **Easy**
PARKING: **A public parking lot is hidden beneath Portsmouth Square.**
PUBLIC TRANSIT: **15 Muni bus**

There is little disputing that San Francisco got off to a spectacular start. By all accounts, the city was thrown up with the purposeful chaos of a carnival pulling into town in the dark of night, and for decades the atmosphere in many parts of town reflected a similar hell's a-poppin' spirit. The area between the main plaza and the wharves distinguished itself and became known as the Barbary Coast.

The name suggested a likeness to the pirate-infested coast of North Africa, where European sailors risked being captured and enslaved on corsair galleys. And indeed San Francisco's Barbary Coast was bad news—for the gullible and the greedy alike. The district was a maze of midways, each block lined with gambling dens, whorehouses, music halls, saloons, and boardinghouses. It was flypaper for sin-seeking sailors.

Serious consequences awaited those who were outsmarted here. The neighborhood was rife with swindlers and shanghaiers. For the miner or shore-leave sailor, the path of least resistance generally led to a knock-out blow in the back room of a saloon. Pacific St., the main stem, was popularly known as "Terrific Street." The district began to form with the arrival of the first Forty-niners and thrived until the devastating quake and fire of 1906.

● **We'll start in Portsmouth Square, which during the Gold Rush was the city's main plaza. City Hall stood on Kearny St. from 1852 to 1895. It occupied the former Jenny Lind Theater (so named in honor of the "Swedish Nightingale," who never performed in San Francisco). Next door was a grand gambling hall called El Dorado. The legendary Bella Union, most popular of the city's music halls, stood on Washington St., just above Kearny. The square itself was a barren patch of earth crisscrossed by footpaths.**

This is where things happened in early San Francisco. In July 1846, the Stars and Stripes were raised here by Captain John B. Montgomery, formally claiming the settlement of Yerba Buena (dubbed San Francisco a year later) for the U.S. A plaque commemorates the event. The square soon acquired the name of Montgomery's ship, the USS *Portsmouth.* Another monument, featuring a cast bronze ship, commemorates a couple of visits by Robert Louis Stevenson, author of the classic tale *Treasure Island.* Having spent a few months in San Francisco in 1879, Stevenson returned in 1888 with his new wife. From here they embarked on the extended sea voyage that would end with the author's death in Samoa, six years later. Now firmly part of Chinatown, Portsmouth Square looks nothing like it would have before 1906, but it is as vital as ever. It still attracts gamblers—on pretty much any day of the week you'll spot men gathered around park benches playing fevered games of cards.

● Follow Washington St. in the direction of the bay, cross Columbus Ave., and you're entering the Jackson Square Historic District. The area has that dignified historic-district air about it, with quiet antique stores and designer furniture showrooms, but don't be fooled. Most of the brick structures here date to the 1850s and '60s, when this area was the city's exciting and dangerous nightlife zone.

● The Transamerica Pyramid (which we examined in the Financial District walk) stands on a historic site, that of the legendary Montgomery Block, commonly known as "Monkey Block." As landmarks that are no longer there go, this one was a doozy. Built in 1853, the Block was for a time the largest and most prestigious commercial building on the West Coast, but it's not for commerce that it is remembered. A bar on the ground floor, called the Bank Exchange, gave the city its signature drink—pisco punch. Pisco was a Peruvian brandy, and pineapple and lime juice were added, along with sugar and other ingredients, to make a syrupy punch that was innocuous in flavor but packed a whallop. It was commonly observed that the drink could "make a gnat fight an elephant." The bar was done in by the Volstead Act in 1919, and the drink was long ago supplanted by margaritas and lychee martinis. As the city grew, the building's more status-conscious tenants moved down Montgomery St., and artists, tradespeople, musicians, writers, and poets moved in. By the 1880s, the Monkey Block was the center of the city's bohemian life. In the basement was a public bath, habituated by writers such as the young Mark Twain, who worked as a reporter in town from 1864–66. (Twain, having deserted the Confederate Army in 1861, spent much of the '60s in the West.) While bathing here Twain reputedly made the acquaintance of a fireman named Tom Sawyer—and, obviously he thought well enough of the name to use it in his best-known work. Ambrose Bierce, Jack London, and Robert Louis Stevenson all either worked in the building or had other excuses for dropping by. The building was demolished in 1959, and the site served as a parking lot for more than a decade before ground was broken for the Transamerica Pyramid.

- Turn left onto Montgomery St. This first block has numerous landmark buildings, most obvious being the Old Transamerica Building (701 Montgomery St.), a flatiron clad in white terra-cotta tiles. It was built in 1911 for A.P. Gianini, founder of the Bank of Italy, which grew to become Bank of America. It's now San Francisco headquarters for the Church of Scientology.

- Across the street, at 710 Montgomery, the Black Cat Cafe was a famous hangout for gays and arty bohemians from 1933 until 1963. In the 1950s, drag-queen host(ess) José Sarria gained notoriety for his operatic performances here. A few doors down, at 716–720 Montgomery, Diego Rivera and Frida Kahlo lived and worked in fellow artist Ralph Stackpole's studios on and off throughout the 1930s. The completely gutted building at 722 Montgomery (it's being rebuilt behind the original facade) was the office of lawyer Melvin Belli from 1959 to 1989. Belli represented Lenny Bruce, Zsa Zsa Gabor, and Errol Flynn, and he added to his infamy by helping to broker the deal that brought the Rolling Stones to the Altamont Speedway in 1969. Scenes in Belli's office are included in the film *Gimme Shelter.* Belli was a flamboyant character who kept a human skeleton named Elmer in his office.

Hotaling Buildings with the Transamerica Pyramid in the background

The building was allowed to deteriorate after the 1989 Loma Prieta earthquake, and its roof eventually caved in, sealing its fate.

- Turn right at Jackson St., and half a block down you'll reach the Hotaling Buildings (455 and 463–73 Jackson), which flank narrow Hotaling Place. Anson Parson Hotaling, who distributed liquor among other goods, built the stately offices at 455 Jackson, then bought the second building, which he used as a warehouse for his booze. When the buildings survived the 1906 quake and fire, a smarmy little rhyme was composed by one Charles K. Field:

  If, as one says, God spanked the town
  For being overfrisky
  Why did He burn the churches down
  And save Hotaling's whisky?

- The building at 415–31 Jackson St. was built in 1853 and once was home to Domingo Ghirardelli's chocolate company. In 1860, Ghirardelli added the structure at 407 Jackson. The older building, you'll notice, has some intriguing details, with faces watching out from the frames of the upstairs windows. The much plainer 1860 building seems to suggest Ghirardelli had his mind more on the bottom line as his business expanded.

- At Sansome St., turn left and then cut back up Gold St. Considering San Francisco owed its good fortune to the Gold Rush, it's interesting that Gold St. should turn out to be a modest lane one block long. Much of it appears to be walled in by the back sides of brick buildings. One entrance leads to Bix, a spectacularly swank supper club that recreates the decadence and grandeur of the Jazz Age.

- Turn right on Montgomery, then left onto Pacific St. It's an agreeable enough street to look at, with its perfectly silent historic buildings, but there's little to suggest how terrific the 400 and 500 blocks were a century ago. We'll just saunter up the 500 block for a peek into the entry of No. 555, graced by some lovely nudes embossed in plaster. Think of this detail as an overt tribute to the neighborhood's bawdy past. The building was once the location of the Hippodrome, a dance hall. The Hippodrome was across the street during its heyday, and moved to this location in time for World

War II. The neighborhood enjoyed a minor revival during the war years, thanks to the influx of military personnel embarking from the city.

● At the junction of Pacific, Kearny, and Columbus, look across Columbus and you'll spot the San Francisco Brewing Company, a brewpub with a past. Go on over, order a pint of the home brew, and inspect the lovingly restored interior, which features a flame-mahogany bar, stained-glass window details, old mosaic tile floors, and a mechanical, rotating, oar-like contraption that, it turns out, is a punka walla ceiling fan. Also note the gutter on the floor, called a spittoon but looking uncomfortably like a latrine. This place opened in 1907 as the Andromeda Saloon, and for the past 80 years or so the barkeeps here have been trying to convince the world that heavy-weight champ Jack Dempsey began his career as a bouncer here. They also will tell you that gangster Baby Face Nelson was captured by the FBI in this bar. Nice try on both counts. But without question, this is a genuinely historic and beautiful place in which to toddle some suds.

● Head north up Kearny toward Broadway. We're entering modern sleazeville, with Kearny a lusterless adjunct of the Broadway strip-tease strip. You'll notice the Lusty Lady, a rare worker-owned strip joint. In the 1990s, the strippers here unionized and went on strike, and in 2003 they bought their bosses out. Apart from that, the place has an old-fashioned peep-show quality, with women behind glass putting on private shows for paying customers, who plop quarters into a slot to keep the show going.

● At Broadway turn left. From the signs above the shops here, it is obvious that this is a very sex-minded street. Broadway looks great at night, when the neon obliterates the darkness overhead. At the corner of Broadway and Columbus, the Condor Club is no longer a strip joint, but the place has retained its name because it was the Taj Mahal of the '60s burlesque scene. Carol Doda's topless and bottomless act set the pace here. A plaque on the Columbus St. side of the building makes hay out of two landmark dates: June 16, 1964, when Ms. Doda first unveiled her ample bosom (which, with silicone enhancement, reputedly reached size 44D); and September 3, 1969, when she first shimmied out of her skivvies on stage. The Condor was also the site of a grizzly death, of the sort that makes people try not to snicker. One night after hours, in November 1983, dancer Theresa Hill and bouncer Jimmy Ferrozzo played hide the salami on top of a piano. The piano was set on a hydraulic lube-like contraption, to make it rise and fall during performances. One thing leading to another, as you might expect, the love-makers were crushed between the piano and the ceiling. The dancer survived. The bouncer didn't. The place is a New Orleans seafood restaurant now.

POINTS OF INTEREST

Bix 56 Gold St., 415-433-6300

Lusty Lady 1033 Kearny St., 415-391-3991

San Francisco Brewing Company 155 Columbus Ave., 415-434-3344

route summary

1. Start at Portsmouth Square, corner of Kearny and Washington streets.
2. Turn right and head east down Washington St., to the intersection of Montgomery St. and Columbus Ave.
3. Turn left on Montgomery St.
4. Turn right on Jackson St.
5. Turn left on Sansome St.
6. Turn left on Gold St.
7. Turn right on Montgomery St.
8. Turn left on Pacific Ave.
9. At the intersection of Kearny St. and Columbus Ave., cross Columbus.
10. Return to corner of Kearny St. and Pacific Ave., make a left and head north, up Kearny, toward Broadway.
11. Turn left on Broadway.
12. End at the corner of Broadway and Columbus Ave.

Old Transamerica Building

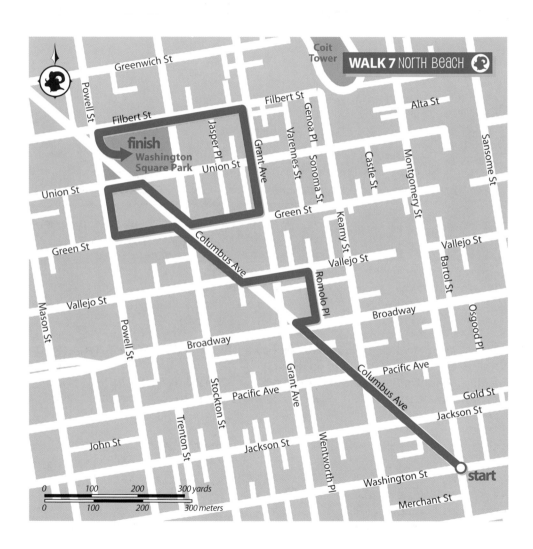

Coit Tower

Greenwich St

Powell St

Filbert St

Jasper Pl

finish
Washington
Square Park

Union St

Filbert St

Genoa Pl

Varennes St

Sonoma St

Grant Ave

Alta St

Castle St

Montgomery St

Sansome St

Union St

Green St

Green St

Kearny St

Vallejo St

Bartol St

Columbus Ave

Vallejo St

Romolo Pl

Broadway

Osgood Pl

Mason St

Vallejo St

Powell St

Broadway

Stockton St

Pacific Ave

Grant Ave

Pacific Ave

Columbus Ave

Gold St

Jackson St

Trenton St

John St

Jackson St

Wentworth Pl

Washington St

start

Merchant St

0   100   200   300 yards

0   100   200   300 meters

7 NORTH BEACH: BOPPIN' DOWN THE BEAT PATH

BOUNDARIES: **Washington St., Powell St., Filbert St., Grant Ave.**
DISTANCE: **1 mile**
DIFFICULTY: **Easy**
PARKING: **There is an underground lot beneath Portsmouth Square, at Washington and Kearny streets, one block from the starting point.**
PUBLIC TRANSIT: **15 and 41 Muni buses.**

North Beach no longer swarms with the goatee-and-beret crowd, and the Italian language is less commonly heard in the neighborhood than it once was. And yet the neighborhood continues to benefit from its heritage as an enclave of Beatniks and Italian immigrants. The chief links to the past are cafes and historic bars, which retain a somewhat earthy, European charm that no doubt appealed to the poets and painters of the Eisenhower years. Italian-American families still own most of the businesses, many of them after several generations. The off-kilter, diagonal slice of the main drag, Columbus Ave., and the closeness of Russian and Telegraph Hills, which rise above North Beach, make this quarter feel more intimate and self-contained than other parts of San Francisco. It's somewhat touristy, especially on weekends. Drop in on a weekday afternoon, or in time for lunch, and you'll get a more local sense of the area. Return at night and take the North Beach Barhopping Tour.

● Start at the foot of Columbus Ave., where the Financial District abruptly ends and North Beach gradually cranks up. Heading north, we'll just mainline it into the neighborhood. The first sign of North Beach character is Caffè Macaroni, a cramped little Italian restaurant at No. 59, where the waiters are notorious for making passes at women who pass by.

● On the next block, the basement-level Purple Onion has been a neighborhood mainstay since 1952. Legendary comedy and folk-music acts have taken its stage. Phyllis Diller and the Kingston Trio got their starts here. Jim Nabors sang in the club in his pre-Gomer days, and the owner, Bud Steinhoff, was in the habit of smashing glass when Nabors reached for high notes. In the 1970s, Robin Williams worked the stage for tips. After a spell as a rock club, the Onion is once again dedicated to comedy.

- On the triangle formed by intersecting Columbus and Kearny stands the green, copper-clad Columbus Tower, headquarters for Francis Ford Coppola's filmmaking company, Zoetrope. Coppola bought the building in 1972, the year his film *The Godfather* was released. Coppola was already a fixture in the neighborhood, frequenting local bars and cafes. He still keeps an office on the top floor, beneath the building's graceful cupola. (Incidentally, a *coppola,* in Italian, is a type of cap once popular amongst the common folk of Sicily.) Cafe Zoetrope, on the ground floor, is a fine spot for a pizza and a bottle of wine. Columbus Tower, originally called the Sentinel Building, was built for corrupt political boss Abe Reuf just after the '06 quake.

- A block up, Jack Kerouac Alley is named for the author of *On the Road* and other stream-of-consciousness tomes that captured the restlessness of the Beat Generation. It's a perfect alley for Kerouac, who liked to drink at Vesuvio, the bar that overlooks the alley. He also associated with poet Lawrence Ferlinghetti, whose City Lights bookstore is just across the alley. Ferlinghetti opened the shop in 1953. He made headlines in 1956 when he published a little pocket edition of Allen Ginsberg's *Howl* and the poem was banned for containing obscenities. Ferlinghetti won a high-profile court battle and the book was put back on the shelves. City Lights is a great bookstore, so step inside and head upstairs to the intimate "Poetry Room," where volumes of verse—Beat or otherwise—fill the shelves. Ferlinghetti's office is just off this little reading room, so you might even run into him.

- At Broadway, on the northwest corner, take a look at the *Jazz* mural, by Bill Weber and Tony Klaas. Clarinetist Benny Goodman (who was not a local figure) presides over a group of San Francisco characters, including Emperor Norton, Herb Caen, and some Italian fishermen.

- Turn right on Broadway. A block down, on the north side, step into the Beat Museum, which is still a work in progress. Drop in to look at Beat memorabilia and a collection of old editions by Kerouac, Ginsberg, Burroughs, and other Holy Goofs. Charles Bukowski is also featured, though he was not really part of the Beat movement. Admission is $5. In the gift shop you can grab hip T-shirts and buttons declaring your Beatitude.

- Head left, up narrow Romolo Place for a look at North Beach's back-alley side, and turn left on Vallejo St. At Grant Ave., make a caffeine stop at Caffè Trieste, a historic coffeehouse that has been run by Giovanni Giotta since 1956. Giotta once aspired to sing opera, and he and his family still sing cantos in the small cafe on Saturday afternoons (twice monthly—call ahead). Trieste has a comfortable, timeworn feel to it, and literary types have always dropped in to kick-start their muses. Francis Ford Coppola worked on his *Godfather* screenplay at one of the tables. The walls are covered with old photos. It's part family album, part celebrity schmoozefest—well worth studying over a cappuccino.

- At Vallejo and Columbus, the church of St. Francis of Assisi was built in 1860. It's the second oldest Catholic church in the city, after the Mission Dolores. Kitty-corner from the church, at 373 Columbus, Molinari Delicatessen is a classic deli, offering hanging salamis, shelves of olives and table wines, and the tantalizing scent of dry cheese. Drop in for a whiff or to grab a sandwich, if you have visions of a picnic at the park later on. (This tour ends at a park.)

- Follow Columbus to Green St. and turn left. At No. 649, the Green Street Mortuary is notable for providing a marching band that leads funeral corteges through Chinatown. The marching band, led by Lisa Pollard, a.k.a. "The Sax Lady," includes many local jazz musicians and even some members of the San Francisco Symphony. If they happen to be marching out as you pass by, quit this tour and follow the band, man.

- Across the street, take note of the Club Fugazi, the attractive theater at

Columbus Tower

No. 678. The zany send-up stage productions of *Beach Blanket Babylon* have ruled the stage here since 1975. Years before that, the Beats put on poetry readings in the club. Next door, Capp's Corner is a friendly old neighborhood eatery that manages to hang on, despite changing tastes.

● Turn right on Powell St. and right again on Union St. Cross Columbus and turn right. This block is one of the street's busiest, alive with cafes and restaurants, including Caffè Roma, where the beans are roasted on the premises, and Rose Pistola, where contemporary Italian is served amid stylish, jazzy decor. No gut-busting portions here.

● Turn left on Green St. Halfway up the block, on the left side, is Danilo Bakery, a family-run establishment that typifies the way in which North Beach retains its intimate, old-world feel. The original owners, Danilo and Danila DiPiramo retired, and rather than close the shop they sold it to another couple, Walter and Stefania Gambaccini, in 2005. It's a fine place for fresh loaves of bread or cookies that are not too sweet.

● Turn left on Grant Ave., which plays second fiddle to Columbus Ave., but does so with a grace that should be instantly apparent. The narrow street is packed with shop fronts of all varieties, including clothing boutiques, antique dealers, grocers, and hardware stores. And, of course, there are a few restaurants, cafes, and bars in the mix. Study the window displays as you walk by, and duck in wherever your curiosity is piqued. Be sure to make it all the way up to Aria, between Union and Filbert. This chaotic and densely packed antique store is like an old curiosity shop. The owner leads a pretty charmed life, spending half the year traveling the globe in search of interesting things to sell in this cluttered store. There's no telling what you might find on any given visit, but the stock tends to range the realm of the unusual and unexpected. Take a look.

● At Filbert St. turn left and walk down toward Washington Square. On the corner of Stockton, poke your head into Liguria, an admirably nondescript shop that sells just one thing: focaccia. In the age of one-stop shopping, this place constitutes the ultimate anachronism, but it manages to get by on the strength of a truly quality product.

If you've been assembling the fixings for a picnic along this tour, be sure to add a warm half-sheet to your sack of victuals.

● Also overlooking the park are Moose's, a busy restaurant that always feels like it's the center of local society, and the church of Saints Peter and Paul. No doubt the church founders shared a round of Peter and Paul jokes when they decided on the name. Crazily, the church's address is 666 Filbert St. It was built in 1924, and is very popular for weddings. Poet Ferlinghetti dubbed it the "marzipan church," and indeed its façade does have a cake-like aspect. Joe DiMaggio and Marilyn Monroe, unable to wed in the church due to an earlier Monroe divorce, snapped their wedding photos on the front steps anyway. (They officially tied the knot at City Hall.)

● The square itself is an odd-shaped square, as diagonal Columbus Ave. slices off the western half of it. But it's a nice patch of green with some trees and statues. Most interesting is the statue of Benjamin Franklin, erected in 1897 by a dentist named Henry D. Cogswell. Cogswell, an ardent prohibitionist, wasn't so much intent on honoring Franklin as he was on luring the town's heavy drinkers away from the bottle. Around the statue's base are water taps, with labels indicating the waters' sources—one indicates the water is from Vichy, France. The spouts have been out of order for decades now. Also in the square is a firemen's statue, put here by fire chaser Lillie Hitchcock Coit. (See the Telegraph Hill walk for more on her.) Pick a bench or a spot on the grass and settle in for a while. Your dogs must be tired.

POINTS OF INTEREST

Caffè Macaroni 59 Columbus Ave., 415-956-9737

Purple Onion 140 Columbus Ave., 415-956-1610

Beat Museum 540 Broadway, 800-537-6822

Molinari Delicatessen 373 Columbus Ave., 415-421-2337

Capp's Corner 1600 Powell St., 415-989-2589

Rose Pistola 532 Columbus Ave., 415-399-0499

Danilo Bakery 516 Green St., 415-989-1806

Aria 1522 Grant Ave., 415-433-0219

Liguria 1700 Stockton St., 415-421-3786

Moose's 1652 Stockton St., 415-989-7800

Sts. Peter and Paul Church 666 Filbert St., 415-421-0809

ROUTE SUMMARY

1. Begin at the southern end of Columbus Ave. and head north, into the neighborhood. 2. Turn right at Broadway.
3. Head left up Romolo Place.
4. Turn left at Vallejo St.
5. Turn right at Columbus Ave.
6. Turn left at Green St.
7. Turn right at Powell St.
8. Turn right at Union St.
9. Turn right at Columbus Ave.
10. Turn left at Green St.
11. Turn left at Grant St.
12. Turn left at Filbert St.
13. Walk to Washington Square, corner of Stockton and Filbert streets.

Vesuvio's self-deprecating sign

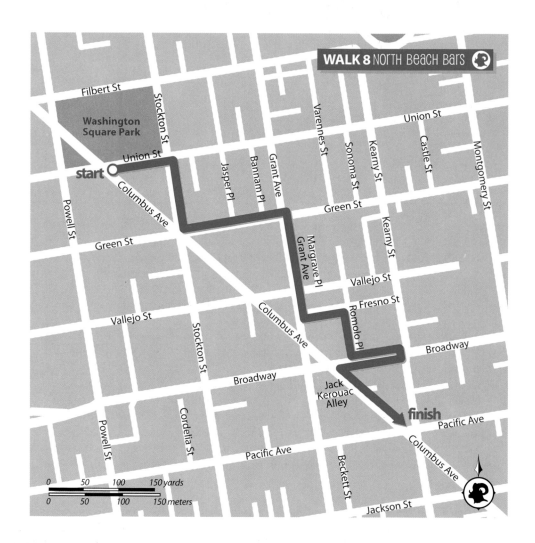

WALK 8 NORTH BEACH Bars

Filbert St

Washington
Square Park

Stockton St

Union St

start

Columbus Ave

Powell St

Jasper Pl

Bannam Pl

Grant Ave

Varennes St

Sonoma St

Kearny St

Union St

Castle St

Montgomery St

Green St

Green St

Margrave Pl
Grant Ave

Kearny St

Vallejo St

Vallejo St

Fresno St

Stockton St

Columbus Ave

Romolo Pl

Broadway

Broadway

Jack
Kerouac
Alley

finish

Pacific Ave

Powell St

Cordelia St

Pacific Ave

Beckett St

Columbus Ave

Jackson St

0   50   100   150 yards
0   50   100   150 meters

8 NORTH BEACH BARS: IN SEARCH OF THE 90-PROOF MUSE

BOUNDARIES: **Union St., Columbus Ave., Grant Ave., Jack Kerouac Alley**
DISTANCE: **Approx. ¾ mile**
DIFFICULTY: **Easy (and getting easier)**
PARKING: **Driving is not a good idea if you're drinking, but there is a parking lot on Vallejo between Columbus Ave. and Mason St.**
PUBLIC TRANSIT: **The 15, 30, and 41 Muni buses all pass through North Beach.**

North Beach is one of San Francisco's best neighborhoods for barhopping, simply because the district contains a variety of fine watering holes within a small, walkable area. The offerings range from rowdy locals to historic Beatnik dives, and the crowds tend to be a diverse mix of city slickers, sozzled poets, and chatty tourists. Surely you'll want to stop and join them here and there. If on occasion you choose to do the lawyerly thing—passing the bar instead of drinking in it—have a vicarious libation and be sure to return for the real thing another time. The best time to hit the bars in North Beach is the latter half of the week, when things are on the upswing, but not on the weekend, when non-locals invade the neighborhood.

- Mario's Bohemian Cigar Store, on the corner of Columbus Ave. and Union St., is always a good place to start for its central location and its early hours. Mario's is a friendly joint with a limited menu, so you can get some carbohydrates under your belt here. The toasted focaccia sandwiches are excellent. It gets its name from the late Mario Crismani, a retired cop from Trieste, Italy, who opened the place in 1972. You'll spot photos of him and his family above the bar. Signore Mario also served as president of the city's Bocce Ball Association. The bar once really did sell cigars, and it was originally a hangout for older Italian gents. These days, the crowd is younger and more mixed, and of course there is no smoking. Other than that, the place hasn't changed a bit.

- After departing Mario's, saunter east, on down Union St. to Stockton St. and turn right. Midway up the block is a classy little joint called Tony Nik's. If you didn't know any better, you'd think this spot was a smart little retro knockoff. But Tony Nik's ain't no knockoff. The decor is of genuine Rat Pack vintage; however, most of Tony Nik's current regulars were born after Frank traded in his brown toupee for a silver one. Many of them insist the only time to come is for Happy Hour (4–7 p.m.), but if "Shellac Shack" is still happening here (first Monday night each month) you might want to drop in later to hear DJ Chas Gaudi spin from his collection of sweet-sounding 78 rpm records.

● At Green St., hook left and in less than a block you'll reach Gino and Carlo, one of North Beach's enduring neighborhood bars. This place is purely local, in the best possible way. It's nothing fancy but always lively, and newcomers will feel welcome. It has some history, too. Long ago, hard-drinking *Chronicle* columnist Charles McCabe—known as the "Fearless Spectator"—regularly penned his daily column from a table here. And rock singer Janis Joplin reputedly frequented the bar in the '60s. The drinks are relatively cheap, there's a pool table and pinball machine, and usually there's a game on T.V.

● At Grant Ave., turn right and head for the Saloon, just past Vallejo St. It's the oldest surviving bar in San Francisco, having opened its doors in 1861. Originally called Wagner's Beer Hall, it is a true survivor—it has endured the demise of the Barbary Coast, the '06 quake, the Prohibition era, and the 1960s. Most of the tosspots who patronize the place are survivors of one kind or another as well. The Saloon, bless it, is no model of gentrification. It's dusty, sagging, and peeling. The faded painted ladies hanging over the bar lack Victorian propriety. But the overall vibe is good. Most nights the Saloon is a blues club, and bands perform here on Sunday afternoon as well.

● Turn left onto narrow Fresno St. and then right on Romolo Place. A sultry little hideaway that opened in the late 1990s, 15 Romolo is both its address and its name. Before that, the place was a Basque restaurant. There are no pretensions here—unless you consider martinis and cosmos pretentious. Otherwise, 15 Romolo is just a solid, friendly spot with a contemporary jukebox selection.

● Romolo Place leads to Broadway, with its garish neon signs and strip-show barkers. You'll notice they don't make barkers like they used to. These guys and dolls don't bark much, but they don't bite either. Enrico's, just half a block to the left, is a North Beach institution that opened in 1959. It's a restaurant with a lively front patio, and unfortunately at this writing it is closed. The place has had earlier hiatuses, and we're hoping this closure also turns out to be temporary.

- Backtrack to Columbus. Hopefully you've still got your legs beneath you, because we're taking the fireworks approach and have saved the biggest splash for last. Turn left, and left again on the squib of a street called William Saroyan Place (named after the author). If you can't find Specs', my friend, you're finished. Wave down a cab. Hopefully that's not the case. Specs' is a little grotto that oozes atmosphere without trying much. Someone took the trouble to outfit the place with curios from every port of the South Seas, but that was decades ago. The place is a dark and dusty museum of the best possible sort, filled with the lurid and the arcane. The crowd is a jovial mix of juiced philosophers and loosened-tie types.

- Just beyond William Saroyan Place is Tosca. Like any great bar or church, Tosca has been around forever and attracts a healthy cross-section of society. The place has a slightly aloof dignity. A sepia hue lingers over the ceiling from decades of cigarette smoke, the old jukebox plays only Italian arias, and the red leatherette booths show very little wear despite their obvious mid-20th century vintage. Bob Dylan and Allen Ginsberg were thrown out of the bar in 1965 after a companion walked into the ladies' room, but these days Tosca is far more accommodating to its celebrity patrons. Sean Penn and Francis Ford Coppola often entertain in the clubby back room.

- On the opposite side of Columbus Ave., two Beat landmarks, Vesuvio and City Lights Bookstore, flank narrow Jack Kerouac Alley. They don't serve drinks at City Lights, so bop on over to Vesuvio. It's a beauty of a bar,

The Saloon

looking much like a Galway pub, though surely that was never intended. The place has its own native eccentricity and a place in North Beach history. It opened in 1949, and when in town, writers such as Kerouac and poet Dylan Thomas drank and told brilliant fish tales here. Owner Henri Lenoir traded in on the Beatnik craze by marketing a kit that included a beret and a false goatee. The place still has the spirit. Sit downstairs to soak in the bar's history or at an upstairs window to watch Columbus Ave. flow by.

POINTS OF INTEREST

Mario's Bohemian Cigar Store 566 Columbus Ave.; 415-362-0536

Tony Nik's 1534 Stockton St.; 415-693-0993

Gino and Carlo 548 Green St.; 415-421-0896

Saloon 1232 Grant Ave.; live music cover $2-5; 415-989-7666

15 Romolo 15 Romolo Place; 415-398-1359

Enrico's 504 Broadway

Specs' 12 William Saroyan Place; 415-421-4112

Tosca Cafe 242 Columbus Ave.; 415-391-1244

Vesuvio 255 Columbus Ave.; 415-362-3370

route summary

1. Begin at Mario's, corner of Union St. and Columbus Ave.

2. Head east, down Union St. to Stockton St. and turn right to reach Tony Nik's.

3. Turn left at Green St. to reach Gino and Carlo's.

4. Turn right at Grant Ave. to reach the Saloon.

5. Turn left at Fresno St.

6. Turn right at Romolo Place to reach 15 Romolo Place.

7. Turn left at Broadway to reach Enrico's.

8. Backtrack on Broadway to Columbus Ave. and turn left.

9. Turn into William Saroyan Place for Specs.'

10. Stay on Columbus Ave. for Tosca.

11. Cross Columbus Ave. and walk to Jack Kerouac Alley to reach Vesuvio.

Pfeiffer St

Chestnut St

Fielding St

Lombard St

Grant Ave

Stockton St

Powell St

Lombard St

Child St

Lombard St

Edith St

Greenwich St

Pioneer Park

Greenwich Steps

Greenwich St

Battery St

Lombard St

Coit Tower

Filbert St

Filbert St

start

Filbert St

Filbert St

Genoa Pl

Kearny St

Alta St

Calhoun Ter

Sansome St

Icehouse Aly

Washington Square Park

Varennes St

Sonoma St

Castle St

Union St

Union St

Columbus Ave

Jasper Pl

Grant Ave

Bannam Pl

Green St

Montgomery St

Vallejo St

Powell St

Green St

finish

Vallejo St

Bartol St

Stockton St

Vallejo St

Fresno St

Kearny St

Columbus Ave

Broadway

Pacific Ave

0   100   200   300 yards

0   100   200   300 meters

9 TeLeGraPH HILL: SCALING THE STairWays To ParaDISE

BOUNDARIES: Stockton St., Greenwich St., Sansome St., Vallejo St.
DISTANCE: 1½ miles
DIFFICULTY: Strenuous
PARKING: Off-street parking is available on Vallejo St., between Stockton and Powell streets, opposite the police station. Curbside parking is very difficult to find and limited to two hours Monday through Saturday.
PUBLIC TRANSIT: 15, 30, 41, and 45 Muni buses

On most days Telegraph Hill feels like San Francisco's Shangri-La, with its wooden stairways zigzagging up hills too steep for paved streets. Walkers are naturally drawn to the steps, which weave through dense gardens and past Victorian houses both humble and refined. This little refuge tells us the rest of San Francisco hasn't taken full advantage of its spectacularly impractical topography. Telegraph Hill wasn't always so pretty a spot, however. Its east face was once a rock quarry overlooking a fleet of rotting ships. By the early 20th century, the hillside had become a de facto dumping ground. Since the 1950s, mostly through tasteful and imaginative landscaping, the hill's once bohemian inhabitants have transformed their hidden quarter. The neighborhood is fairly hoity now, thanks to escalating real estate values, but it continues to offer the city's best walking. A good time to walk this one is on a lightly overcast morning, when details are drawn out from the shadows beneath the trees.

● **The hill slopes up from North Beach, so we'll start at Washington Square, on the corner of Filbert and Stockton streets, and walk a block over to Greenwich. Just before you reach Greenwich, the arts and crafts Swiss chalet at 1736 Stockton is the Maybeck Building. Berkeley-based Bernard Maybeck, one of California's most influential architects, designed the building in 1907. It was originally the Telegraph Hill Neighborhood House, which offered services to immigrant families. Enter into a shady courtyard, which is a pleasant composition consisting of a brick patio surrounded by varying inner faces of the building.**

- At Greenwich St., turn right and head up (and up and up). At Grant Ave., turn right, and half a block down, at Gerte Alley, you'll get an attractive preview of Coit Tower. It's a more than adequate excuse for breaking up the upward trek. Back on Greenwich head up the steps through Pimentell Garden, named for Samantha Pimentell, who tended the flora here for 25 years. The steps lead to Telegraph Hill Blvd., on which cars spiral up to the summit. Rather than follow the road, look on the other side for the stone steps that lead to the top.

- Pioneer Park, on the leveled summit of Telegraph Hill, is where you'll find Coit Tower and also a statue of Christopher Columbus, which was a gift from Columbus' hometown of Genoa, Italy. The explorer, who for better or worse got so many things rolling in the Americas, never laid eyes on San Francisco Bay, but this bronze likeness appears to be admiring the view of it. You ought to do the same. The vantage here is as wide as it gets, ranging from the Golden Gate to the west and on past Treasure Island to the east. In the early days of San Francisco, the arrival of ships entering the Golden Gate was observed from this lookout, and through semaphore signals the news, along with the type of ship, was "telegraphed"

BACK STORY: WILD PARROTS

The parrots you're likely to see on Telegraph Hill are cherry-head conures, which first appeared here in the late 1970s or early 1980s. Many were either released or escaped from captivity, but a sizeable portion were born wild in San Francisco. Mark Bittner, author of *The Wild Parrots of Telegraph Hill* and subject of the documentary film of the same name, squatted in a former artist's shack on Greenwich St. for many years, studying and getting to know the birds. The book and film are highly recommended for anyone desiring a fascinating perspective on Telegraph Hill.

(thus the hill's name) to the bustling downtown clustered on Yerba Buena Cove. Touts would sail or row out to meet the ships as they slowly proceeded into the bay. The city's economy revolved around shipping, and the bulk of the population would rush to the docks to greet each ship as it tied in.

● Coit Tower is visible from just about anywhere to the east of Nob and Russian hills, and is one of the city's more puzzling architectural monuments. A fluted column topped by an arched observatory, it was originally derided by locals, who saw it as a sore thumb. San Franciscans are notoriously negative when it comes to new structures invading their skyline, but the city eventually came around to accepting this one. It looks particularly attractive at night, when it's illuminated by lamps beaming up from the ground. It bears the name of Lillie Hitchcock Coit, who funded the project through an endowment specified in her will. Coit (1843–1929) was raised in San Francisco and became a big fan of a company of volunteer firefighters called Knickerbocker Engine Company No. 5. In those days, multiple companies would respond to fire alarms, and it was a competition to see which company arrived at a scene first to put out the fire. Some citizens, such as young Lillie, cheered on their favorite companies much as sports fans today cheer on their favorite teams. Coit's passion for Knickerbocker No. 5 far surpassed the norm, however, and by the age of 20 she had become an honorary member of the company. She considered it a point of honor to appear at every fire along with her beloved crew of smoke-eaters. Consequently, many have speculated that Coit Tower was designed to resemble a fire-hose nozzle, but architect Henry T. Howard always maintained this was not his intention.

Julius' Castle

- You can enter Coit Tower's lobby free of charge to inspect the beautiful WPA murals, which were added a year after the tower's completion in 1933. These frescoes sparked a huge controversy, as many of them have Socialist undertones. Some of the scenes depict laborers struggling to keep up with the demands of industry. Some of the more overt details in the original works were censored before the murals were unveiled. To reach the top, where all downtown San Francisco pops into view, you'll have to pay $4.50 to ride the elevator.

- Exit the tower, descend the front steps, turn right, and look for the street sign for Greenwich St. This leads not to a paved road, but to some brick steps. Follow these down through dense greenery all the way to Montgomery St. Turn left at the bottom of the stairs and you'll reach Julius' Castle, one of the hill's kookier structures. This turreted fortress was the dream child of restaurateur Julius Roz, who opened the establishment in 1922. It's still operating after more than eight decades.

- From the castle, walk along the east side of Montgomery past two buildings and find steps cutting back and then down Greenwich St., a pretty darn peaceful hideaway. The gardens here

BACK STORY: IN THE KITCHEN WITH DYNA

For many years in the late 19th and early 20th century, rock was blasted out of Telegraph Hill's eastern side by a company called the Gray Brothers. Using dynamite, the company regularly shook the foundations of the workingmen's cottages above, and in some instances the blasts actually destroyed homes. The property on the hill, though very central, was affordable to dockhands because the grades were too steep to attract the wealthy. The Gray Brothers intended to continue quarrying until Telegraph Hill was completely flattened, along the way buying out the hill's unfortunate residents at fire sale prices. Once the hill was flattened, real estate values would naturally increase, and the Gray Brothers could then sell the land for top dollar. Telegraph Hill residents fought back, getting a court injunction to stop the blasting, and when the Gray Brothers defied the court, the neighbors rolled rocks down on the company, to slow their progress. Eventually, one of the Gray Brothers was killed by an employee of the company, putting a stop to rock quarrying on Telegraph Hill.

are the main attraction for the neighborhood's flock of parrots, whom you'll often hear squawking in the canopy overhead. At 231 Greenwich you'll see some wood steps to the right. Head up a little ways for an up-close look at some rusticated shacks that reflect the old neighborhood's bohemian past, and then return to the Greenwich Steps and head down to the bottom. At Sansome St., turn right and walk one block to Filbert St. and look to your right.

- From the bottom of Filbert it should be instantly obvious that you have your work cut out for you. A concrete and metal stairway ascends a sheer cliff carved out by rock quarrying in the 19th century. Flowers cling to the cliffside, thanks to adventurous gardeners who rappelled down to plant seedlings.

- From the top of the cliff rustic wood steps lead into the Grace Marchant Gardens, which are the most elaborate and lovingly tended gardens on the hill. Grace Marchant, a retired Hollywood stuntwoman, resided at the corner of Filbert and Napier Lane, where in 1950 she began the gardens that now flourish here. Her daughter, Valletta, took on a similar mission on Greenwich St. Today, the gardens are tended by neighborhood volunteers. The land itself belongs to the city.

- A wood plank walkway is narrow Napier Lane, where we ought to make a short detour, for this is surely the sweetest cul-de-sac in all San Francisco. Little more than a footpath, it accesses a row of small houses shaded by trees. Farther up Filbert, Darrell Place is a similarly narrow, though paved lane.

- At the top of the block, the art deco apartment building at 1360 Montgomery appeared in the 1947 film *Dark Passage,* starring Humphrey Bogart and Lauren Bacall. The building stood in for Bacall's apartment, where she allowed the fugitive Bogart to hide out. Scenes in the neighborhood reveal that the steps weren't nearly so beautiful then as they are today. The silver nautical motifs on the building's side make it instantly recognizable and also make it a good photo op. The film is well worth watching.

- Turn left onto Montgomery St. and left again half a block later, onto historic Alta St. On the south side of the block, the red brick house with upstairs galleries at 31 Alta was a speakeasy during Prohibition. On the north side, the house at 60–64

Alta is known as the "Duck House," for the ducks painted beneath the eaves. Author Armistead Maupin lived in one of the building's apartments in the early 1970s, and actor Rock Hudson reputedly visited him here.

● Alta dead-ends, so backtrack to Montgomery, turn left, and turn left again onto Union St., which leads to a nub called Calhoun Terrace. Here some of the city's oldest houses rub shoulders with modern masterpieces. The Kahn House, at 66 Calhoun, is the work of Richard Neutra, the architect often credited with introducing the International style of modern architecture to California. His cliffhanger doesn't look at all out of place here, and its expansive windows fully exploit the view of the bay. For the best vantage point, walk a little ways down the Union St. steps and look up at Neutra's building. Loop around to the upper side of Calhoun. The house at 9 Calhoun was built in 1854—very early days for this city—and it has been lovingly restored.

● Return to Montgomery St. and meander back down to North Beach. Half a block past Union, Montgomery dead-ends, and the steps leading down afford a perfect perspective of the Transamerica Pyramid and the Financial District skyline. Turn right onto Green St. and left onto Kearny St. For the heck of it, cut down San Antonio Place, which has no sign and looks like an entry to an apartment building's parking garage. It loops through the buildings, opening onto the Vallejo St. steps. Turn right onto Vallejo and it's a straight shot to Caffè Trieste, where an espresso or beer surely has your name on it.

POINTS OF INTEREST

Coit Tower 1 Telegraph Hill Blvd., 415-362-0808
Julius' Castle 1541 Montgomery St., 415-392-2222
Caffè Trieste 601 Vallejo St., 415-392-6739

route summary

1. Start at the corner of Stockton and Filbert streets.

2. Walk one block north on Stockton St.

3. Turn right at Greenwich St.

4. At Grant Ave. turn right and walk half a block to Gerte St., then return to Greenwich St.

5. Walk up to Coit Tower and Pioneer Park.

6. Look for the sign to Greenwich St., at the top of Greenwich Steps, and walk down the steps.

7. At Montgomery St., along the east side of the street, look for the continuation of the Greenwich Steps.

8. At Sansome St., turn right.

9. At Filbert St. turn right, and ascend the steps.

10. Take a quick detour onto Napier Lane.

11. At Montgomery St., turn left.

12. Take a detour onto Alta St. and then continue on Montgomery St.

13. Take a detour onto left, onto Union St. and Calhoun Terrace; then continue on Montgomery St.

14. Turn right onto Green St.

15. Turn left onto Kearny St.

16. Follow San Antonio Place, which leads to the Vallejo Steps.

17. Turn right onto Vallejo, following it down to the corner of Grant Ave.

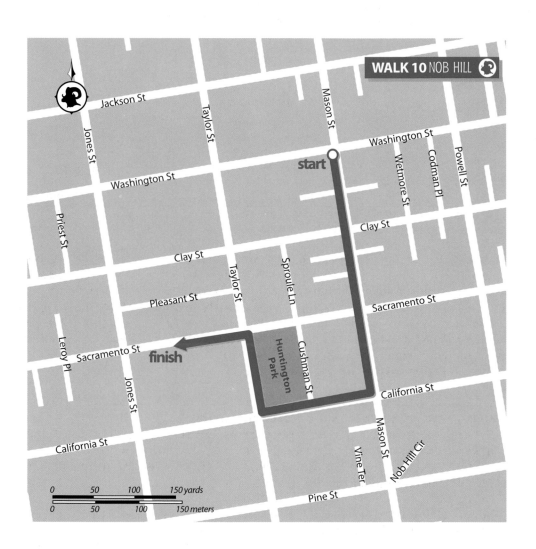

10 NOB HILL: HIGH ALTITUDE HIGH JINX

BOUNDARIES: **Washington St., Mason St., California St., Jones St.**
DISTANCE: **Approx. ¾ mile**
DIFFICULTY: **Mildly Strenuous**
PARKING: **St. Mary's garage, California St. and Grant Ave.**
PUBLIC TRANSIT: **Powell–Mason cable car**

The nabobs and their opulent mansions are long gone, but Nob Hill still has a prestigious air about it. In the 1870s, soon after the advent of cable cars simplified getting up the hill from downtown, the silver kings and railroad barons moved in. Three decades later, the 1906 quake turned their privileged perch into an ash heap. High-class hotels, a lovely park, and awe-inspiring Grace Cathedral now stand where San Francisco's Robber Barons once lived. Add to the mix a handful of unexpected curiosities and you've got yourself a dandy little tour.

● Since Nob Hill began with the development of cable cars, we'll start our tour at the Cable Car Museum, on the corner of Washington and Mason streets. If you're a perfectionist, you can take the Powell-Mason cable car and get off directly in front of the museum. This is more than a historic site—it's the powerhouse that keeps all the cable cars moving. Inside, take a look at the system of wheels that turn the cables like spindles in a cassette tape. These cables run under the tracks of the entire system: the cars move by gripping onto the cables. Exhibits here demonstrate how the system works, and also include some historic cable cars and photos.

● Head up Mason St. for two blocks to reach the summit of Nob Hill. It's all level strolling from here on out. At the corner of Sacramento St., just about everything we've climbed these heights to inspect comes into view. At 1000 Mason St. are the stately Brocklebank Apartments, which feature in the Hitchcock film *Vertigo.* In an early scene, James Stewart, waiting behind the wheel of his car, begins stalking Kim Novak as she emerges from this building.

● Across the street, the imposing Fairmont Hotel is one of many eye-catching buildings on Nob Hill. It's on the site of silver king James Fair's mansion, which was torn down by Fair's daughter before the quake of '06. The hotel she built on the site was nearly completed when the quake and fire turned it into a burned-out hull. Architect Julia Morgan drew the plans to restore the hotel, which finally opened a year to the day after the quake. Enter the Fairmont's grand lobby, have a seat in a plush chair, pretend you're waiting for someone, and admire the marble columns and stately stairs. Then poke around a bit. Peer into the swank Venetian Room restaurant, study the charming, dated murals of circus performers in the otherwise dowdy Cirque Bar, and ride the glass elevator to the top of the Fairmont's tower for a spectacular view. For the hotel's biggest surprise, you'll have to head down to the basement. Here you'll find the Tonga Room, a tiki bar that spared no expense when it came to the decor. Thatched umbrellas cover the tables, drinks are served in plastic coconut shells, and every 30 minutes a simulated monsoon strikes. Time your visit for happy hour and you're likely to forget all about finishing this tour.

● Back outside, keep your ears peeled for the sound of the California St. cable car. It's the oldest of the surviving lines, having begun service April 10, 1878.

● Continue on Mason to California St. At the southeast corner of the Mason and California intersection stands the Mark Hopkins Hotel. Hopkins was among the "Big Four" railroad barons, and his mansion—which photos reveal to have been the hill's most extravagant—stood on this site. The mansion was a quake casualty, but the stone retaining wall survives. Note the way this building and the Brocklebank apartments, a block away, complement one another. The main attraction at the Mark Hopkins is the Top of the Mark, a snazzy bar with 360-degree views, a martini menu that's several pages long, and jazz combos several nights weekly.

● The distinguished brownstone mansion across the street from the Fairmont belonged to James Flood, the shrewd saloon keeper who made his fortune on the Comstock Lode. Walk along California St. to get a good look at it. The 1906 quake and fire failed to bring the mansion down, but it did require significant restoration; Willis Polk designed the additions. The Pacific Union Club, one of the city's most exclusive, has owned the house since 1906.

● Make a left onto California St. Pleasant Huntington Park shares the block with the Flood Mansion. It's a good spot to claim a park bench and study Grace Cathedral, across the street. The park's *Tortoise Fountain* and bronze *Dancing Sprites* sculpture are also worth looking at for perhaps 10 seconds or half a minute. The park also has a swing set, in case you've had a few at the Top of the Mark and still feel like swinging.

● Rather than head directly to Grace Cathedral, cross California St. The Huntington Hotel, another of San Francisco's finest, stands on the southeast corner. Your eye may naturally drift over to the Masonic Memorial Temple, on the southwest corner. Don't fight that impulse. The building isn't exactly beautiful, but it is adorned by some impressive art, most notably the immense 45-by-48-foot "endomosaic" window in the lobby. Artist Emile Norman invented the style, pressing crushed glass, sea shells, soil, and other materials between sheets of translucent plastic. After two years of working on it, he completed it in 1957. It depicts Masonic history in California with typically mysterious symbols and a starkly twisted 1950s style. During business hours you can enter for a close look. It's actually quite fetching when the sun shines through it.

● Now let's have a look at Grace Cathedral. Before entering, pause to inspect the bronze doors, which are lovely copies of Lorenzo Ghiberti's *Doors of Paradise* in Florence, Italy. Tuck in your shirt and go inside. (The cathedral requests a $5 donation.) The Cathedral, lofty enough to stage a dogfight between two small bi-planes (though such a spectacle has yet to occur), was erected on the charred grounds of the mansion of Charles Crocker, a Big Four magnate. The cathedral was designed by Lewis P. Hobart, who studied at the École des Beaux Arts in Paris. Construction began not long after the '06 quake and was completed in 1964. While inside, direct your peepers to the elegant and awesome 25-foot-wide rose window, above the main entrance.

Grace Cathedral

● From here, emerge onto Taylor St., return to Sacramento St., and turn left for a look at some relatively modest, but still eye-pleasing residential architecture. The bougainvillea-clad apartments at 1230 and 1242 Sacramento have an elegant, Belle Époque Parisian style. On the corner of Jones St., at 1298 Sacramento St., the Chambord Apartments are well loved for their extravagant rounded balconies that call to mind Gaudi's ebullient style.

POINTS OF INTEREST

Cable Car Museum 1201 Mason St., 415-474-1887

Fairmont Hotel 950 Mason St., 415-772-5000

Tonga Room 950 Mason St., 415-772-5278

Mark Hopkins Hotel 999 California St., 415-392-3434

Top of the Mark 999 California St., 415-616-6916

Masonic Memorial Temple 1111 California St., 415-776-4702

Grace Cathedral 1100 California St., 415-749-6300

route summary

1. Start at the corner of Mason and Washington streets.
2. Walk up Mason St. to Sacramento St., to the top of Nob Hill.
3. Continue on Mason St. to California St.
4. Turn left on California St.
5. Walk through Huntington Park.
6. At the corner of Taylor and California streets, cross over to the Masonic Temple.
7. Re-cross California St. to Grace Cathedral.
8. Emerge onto Taylor St. and turn left.
9. Turn left on Sacramento St.

Cable Car Museum and cable car

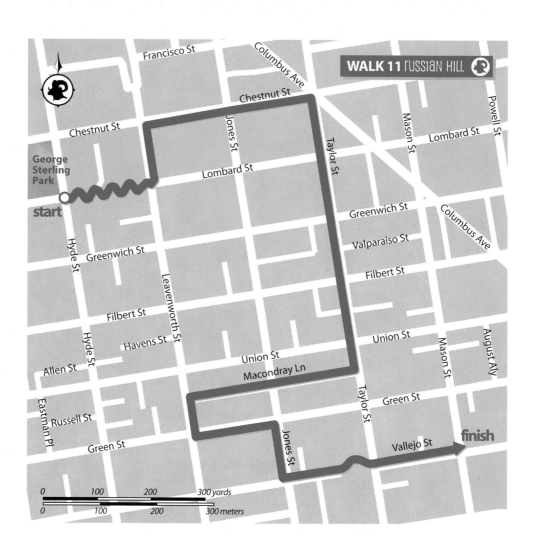

Francisco St

Columbus Ave

Chestnut St

Chestnut St

Jones St

Taylor St

Mason St

Lombard St

Powell St

George
Sterling
Park

Lombard St

start

Hyde St

Greenwich St

Greenwich St

Columbus Ave

Valparaiso St

Filbert St

Leavenworth St

Filbert St

Union St

Havens St

Allen St

Hyde St

Union St
Macondray Ln

Mason St

August Aly

Eastman Pl

Russell St

Green St

Jones St

Taylor St

Green St

Vallejo St

finish

Green St

0   100   200   300 yards

0   100   200   300 meters

11 rUSSian HiLL: PONDEriNG THE CUrVY STrEET DISPUTE (AND HIDING ON HIDDEN HILLTOP LANES)

BOUNDARIES: Hyde St., Lombard St., Mason St., Vallejo St.
DISTANCE: 1¼ miles
DIFFICULTY: Strenuous (steep hills)
PARKING: Street parking is nearly impossible to find and limited to two hours.
PUBLIC TRANSIT: The Hyde St. cable car stops at the starting point of this tour. The Muni 41 Union bus stops at Hyde, just a few blocks away.

Russian Hill is more hilly than it is Russian—in fact, not one fur hat did we see while walking the streets of this part of town while researching this book. (The name supposedly comes from shadowy rumors of Russian sailors who were buried here ages ago.) This was once a bohemian enclave, and it retains much of its quirkiness—in large part due to the neighborhood's uncompromising topography. Russian Hill is not at all conducive to the grid system in which downtown San Francisco's streets are laid out, so some streets simply dead-end, giving way to narrow footpaths and stairwells. This did not stop San Franciscans from building their houses here, and today it seems the more inaccessible the house, the more desirable the property. Gardeners have made the most of the neighborhood's secluded pedestrian zones, and walkers are likely to marvel that such tranquility is to be found so near the dense heart of the city.

● We'll begin at the top of the curvy block of Lombard St.—commonly billed, with sideshow hyperbole, as the "crookedest street in the world." Russian Hill's best known landmark is a tidy, picture-perfect example of urban landscaping. Gardeners tend to yawn at the choice of planting, which looks like the work of a fussy old granny. Meanwhile some locals insist that Lombard isn't even the curviest street in the city. The other candidate, Vermont St. between McKinley and 22nd streets, at the foot of Potrero Hill, has five full turns and two half turns crammed into a single city block. Lombard has eight turns. Decision goes to Lombard. As you walk the curvy steps down, marvel over these facts: the hill has a 27-percent grade; the street originally ran straight down it; the curves were introduced in 1922 to slow cars down and to beautify the street; the postcards began to appear soon after that.

- After negotiating that last curve, turn left onto Leavenworth St. and then right on Chestnut St. The San Francisco Art Institute beckons. It's architecturally interesting, exhibiting the hallmarks of Spanish revival, such as a tower and a courtyard, while being built almost entirely of formed concrete. But the real attraction here is the Diego Rivera Gallery, featuring a fresco by the master himself. Rivera painted it in 1931 and called it *The Making of a Fresco Showing a Building of a City.* You'll notice Rivera painted himself into the scene. The gallery can be reached by walking through the courtyard.

- Continue down Chestnut to Columbus Ave., the Main Street of North Beach. From the corner, you'll spot the marquee of Bimbo's 365 Club, one of the swankiest live music clubs in San Francisco. It's famous for the girl, clad in her birthday suit, who swims for hours in a fishbowl. No one has ever sufficiently explained how she got in the fishbowl, or why she doesn't need to come up for air. Bimbo's has been operating on this spot since 1951, and retains much of its fun, swingin' vibe. In an earlier location, on Market St., a young Rita Hayworth danced in the club's chorus line.

- From this corner make a right on Taylor St. and follow it uphill for several blocks. Stay on the right side of the street. After crossing Union St. be on the lookout on your right for a wooden staircase heading skywards from the sidewalk. This is not a private entrance—it is Macondray Lane, an actual city street (you'll spot the street sign). Climb on up. Macondray inspired author Armistead Maupin's "Barbary Lane" in *Tales of the City.* Stroll the deeply shaded footpath—which switches from wood steps to rough-cut stone to brick—and you'll see why this is one of the least urban streets in the city. It's lined on one side with nondescript Victorian houses, and local gardeners have turned some of the terraced spaces here into jungles of bamboo, tree ferns, and ponds. Ina Coolbrith, a poet and literary socialite, hosted her legendary salon at 15 Macondray Lane during the early 20th century. Coolbrith later had a park named for her, which we'll visit on this tour.

- Follow Macondray past Jones St. to Leavenworth St. and turn left. At Green St. turn left again. This is a historic block, with 12 buildings listed on the National Register. Nearly every house on the south side of the street predates the 1906 earthquake and fire. The obvious standout is number 1067, the Feusier Octagon House. Built in 1857–59, this was one of many eight-sided homes built in San Francisco (another can be seen on the Marina and Cow Hollow Walk). Orson S. Fowler, a phrenologist, developed the idea of octagon houses, saying they let in more light and offered improved ventilation. The mansard roof and dormers were added in the 1880s. The house at 1055 Green was built around 1866. It originally was an unassuming Italianate house, but in 1915 it was completely remodeled by Julia Morgan, who turned it into a Beaux Arts villa with stucco siding and a beautiful cast-iron balcony. Across the street, the charming Swiss Chalet at 1088 Green was originally a firehouse—Engine House No. 31. It was built in 1907.

● Turn right at Jones St. Two ramps to your left link Jones to a short block of Vallejo St., adding to the secluded feel of this charmed cul-de-sac. The ramps, designed by Willis Polk in 1914, were commissioned not by the city but by a wealthy resident of the block. Polk also designed the lovely shingle-sided craftsman house at 1015–19 Vallejo St. For a good vantage of it step into the lawn at the end of the block. From this point, you'll also get a fine view of North Beach far below.

● Continue down the Vallejo St. steps to Taylor St., noting that photographer Dorothea Lange lived in an apartment at No. 1637 for several years during the late 1920s and early '30s. Cross Taylor and enter Ina Coolbrith Park, which, like the steps you've just descended, stands in for what would have been Vallejo St. if the hill hadn't been so steep. A plaque on a rock to the left of the park's entrance tells the story of Coolbrith, a poet who is largely forgotten by today's literati. Meander down the steps, admiring the varying view as you lose altitude. At the bottom, you'll find yourself just a couple of blocks from the heart of North Beach—and at the end of this tour.

Diego Rivera's fresco

POINTS OF INTEREST

San Francisco Art Institute 800 Chestnut St., 415-771-7020

Bimbo's 365 Club 1025 Columbus Ave., 415-474-0365

route summary

1. Begin at the corner of Hyde and Lombard streets, and head down the curvy street.
2. Turn left on Leavenworth St.
3. Turn right on Chestnut St.
4. Turn right on Taylor St.
5. After crossing Union St., turn right and head up steps to Macondray Lane.
6. Turn left on Leavenworth St.
7. Turn left on Green St.
8. Turn right on Jones St.
9. Turn left on Vallejo St.
10. Follow steps down to Taylor St., cross Taylor, and continue down through Ina Coolbrith Park.

Bay windows and view of Alcatraz

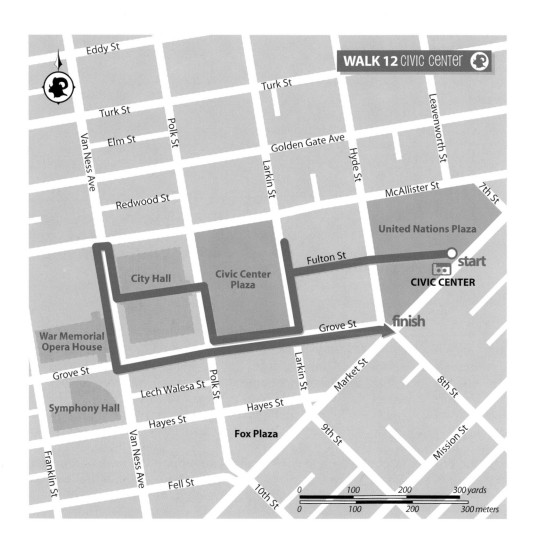

Eddy St

Turk St

Turk St

Elm St

Polk St

Golden Gate Ave

Larkin St

Hyde St

Leavenworth St

McAllister St

7th St

Van Ness Ave

Redwood St

United Nations Plaza

City Hall

Civic Center Plaza

Fulton St

start

CIVIC CENTER

Grove St

finish

War Memorial Opera House

Grove St

Lech Walesa St

Polk St

Larkin St

Market St

8th St

Symphony Hall

Hayes St

Hayes St

Van Ness Ave

Fox Plaza

9th St

Mission St

Franklin St

Fell St

10th St

0   100   200   300 yards

0   100   200   300 meters

12 CIVIC CenTer: Beaux arTs BeauTies anD CaTHeDrals OF CulTure

BOUNDARIES: **Market St., Leavenworth St., McAllister St., Van Ness Ave.**
DISTANCE: **1 mile**
DIFFICULTY: **Easy**
PARKING: **There is an underground parking lot beneath Civic Center Plaza.**
PUBLIC TRANSIT: **Civic Center BART; F streetcars; Market St. Muni buses**

San Francisco's Civic Center is one of the most elegant and cohesively planned complexes in the U.S. Huge monumental Beaux Arts structures went up after the 1906 quake, making the area impressive but cold on the surface. Some of the buildings house offices of government, while others are pillars of high culture and contribute much needed warmth to the neighborhood. The opera, the symphony, the Main Library, and the Asian Art Museum are all clustered around City Hall, which itself is one of the country's finest capitol buildings. The area is always busy, especially on weekdays when local, state, and federal government workers file in and out of the buildings along with museum goers and grade-school students bused in for field trips. On Wednesday and Sunday a farmers' market adds even more life and diversity to the area, making these days ideal for a trek through the neighborhood.

● **Start at United Nations Plaza, at the corner of Market and Leavenworth. Named in commemoration of the 1945 signing of the United Nations Charter near here (see Herbst Theater, below), the Plaza is a somewhat awkward open space that on most days merely serves as a shortcut from Market St. to the library and City Hall. The Heart of the City Farmers' Market changes that on Wednesday and Sunday, when vendors from Northern California farms set up stalls overflowing with produce, nuts, seafood, baked goods, and flowers. It's a lively and upbeat event that contrasts greatly with the down-and-outers who usually congregate around the plaza's fountain. From anywhere in the plaza, you can turn around and see Rigo's *Truth* mural emblazoned on the top floors of a Market St. building. Rigo painted the mural in 2002.**

● **Pass through the plaza and cross Hyde St. Head west, up Fulton St., which separates the Main Library (to the left) and the Asian Art Museum (to the right). In the middle** of the street stands the intriguing Pioneer Monument, commissioned by millionaire James Lick, who made his fortune by playing the real estate game in the Gold Rush city. Lick hired sculptor Frank Happersberger to create a tribute to the Argonauts of that era. Thus, we have this large monument with bronze miners panning for gold beneath the bronze figure of the Roman goddess Minerva, standing on what appears to be a huge granite fire plug.

- The Asian Art Museum occupies the former main library, a Beaux Arts structure originally built in 1917. When the library moved into its current home across the street the old library building was completely gutted and remodeled to accommodate the immense holdings of the Asian Art Museum, which had outgrown its space in Golden Gate Park. The core of the collection was donated to the museum by Avery Brundage, the Chicago developer who also served as president of the International Olympic Committee for two decades. Brundage's huge bequest was the impetus for the founding of the museum and still comprises half the collection. Religious, military, and artistic objects span the entire region, from the Philippines to Iran, and some date back as far as 6,000 years. The architecture is luxuriant inside and out, but you won't be permitted to step in for a peek at the lobby or the gift shop without paying the $10 admission price.

- Retrace your steps and cross Fulton St. to the Main Library, which opened in 1995 to mostly positive reviews. Enter the building on the Larkin St. side and take an elevator to the fifth floor. From here, you can look down the building's central atrium or climb to the top floor via a spiral staircase, which ascends towards a fetching geometric glass ceiling. The library has many reading and research rooms that are worth perusing, including special collections filled with materials relating to the varied ethnic and cultural groups of San Francisco. The top floor is occupied by the excellent San Francisco History Center, which always has an informative exhibit of photos, newspaper clippings, and other items from its collection. Other thoughtful and interesting exhibits, some culled from the History Center, are in the Jewett Gallery, on the basement level of the library.

- Cross Larkin and walk through Civic Center Plaza toward the back of City Hall. The Plaza is remarkable for its plainness, and is often populated by homeless sunbathers. Sometimes you'll catch a huge group of office workers participating in an organized tai chi exercise routine.

● On the Polk St. side of City Hall is a statue of Abraham Lincoln appearing ready to hold a discourse with anyone walking by. Head up the steps and enter City Hall, which is open to anyone not brandishing a firearm or any other dangerous items. San Francisco's City Hall has had a tumultuous past. Its predecessor, which stood where the Asian Art Museum is now, took two decades to build, and soon after its completion it crumbled to the ground in the initial temblor of 1906. It seems shady construction had resulted in a flimsy structure. All that remains of the old City Hall is the head of the Goddess of Progress statue that stood atop its dome (you'll see her in the South Wing exhibit). The current Beaux Arts City Hall was completed in 1915, and there is much to admire about it. The firm of Bakewell and Brown designed it. The dome, lovingly restored during Mayor Willie Brown's tenure, is taller than the Capitol dome in Washington, D.C. Wander the main floor to gaze up at the magnificent rotunda and at the staircase spilling down like the train of a bridal gown. Tragedy came to City Hall in 1978, when Mayor George Moscone and Supervisor Harvey Milk (the city's first openly gay elected official) were shot and killed in their offices by former supervisor Dan White. White's lawyers convinced the jury that he was mentally unstable, and on the night he was convicted of manslaughter rather than murder outraged gays rioted in front of City Hall. The night is remembered as "White Night." On a lighter note, Marilyn Monroe and Joe DiMaggio were married in a civil ceremony in City Hall in 1954. So were some 4,000 same-sex couples in a startling display of civil disobedience in February 2004. Newly elected Mayor Gavin Newsom defied state law by permitting the weddings, and he even presided over some of the ceremonies. Gay brides and grooms lined out the doors of City Hall for weeks, along with an armada of media trucks, clogging up traffic and creating a street-party

San Francisco City Hall

89

atmosphere. Newsom's antics were soon stopped and the state revoked the unions. Have a look around and exit on the Van Ness Ave. side. Turn right and cross Van Ness at McAllister.

● Two nearly identical landmark buildings share the block across the street from City Hall. On the right (north side) is the War Memorial Veterans Building, which was designed by Bakewell and Brown and completed in 1932. Inside, the Herbst Theater is an intimate performance hall that gained renown in June 1945 when the United Nations Charter was signed in a ceremony on its stage. Off the front lobby, the San Francisco Arts Commission Gallery is a never-dull exhibition space for contemporary artists, and admission is free so take a look.

● From Veterans Hall mosey on over to the War Memorial Opera House. The two buildings, which commemorate the soldiers who fought in World War I, were built at the same time, and Arthur Brown Jr. (of Bakewell and Brown) designed the Opera House. G. Albert Lansburgh designed the Opera House's elegant interior. The San Francisco Opera was founded in 1923, and the opening night of each opera season is a big event among opera aficionados and socialites.

● At Grove St., Louise M. Davies Symphony Hall is a modern structure that looks its best on performance nights, when the curved glass facade is ablaze with warm light. The hall was built in 1980 and has housed the city's lauded symphony ever since. If you're a mite peckish or parched, Absinthe Brasserie and Bar is just around the corner, at Hayes and Franklin streets. It's a stylish recreation of a belle époque brasserie where you can slurp raw oysters or traditional French fare.

● Cross Van Ness and walk two blocks on Grove St. The Bill Graham Civic Auditorium faces Civic Center Plaza. Named for the legendary rock-and-roll impresario, Bill Graham, who based his operations in San Francisco, the auditorium is frequently the sight of performances by major rock artists. On the sidewalk in front of the building you'll stroll over a "Walk of Fame," embedded with plaques honoring local music figures.

● At Hyde St. turn right and then turn left onto Market St. You'll immediately notice the flamboyant façade of the Orpheum Theater. Built in 1926, the Orpheum was initially a Pantages Vaudeville hall and then a grand movie palace. Today, it houses Broadway stage productions. Step into the covered entry, elegantly clad in marble. It's still a beauty.

POINTS OF INTEREST

Asian Art Museum 200 Larkin St., 415-581-3500

Main Library 100 Larkin St., 415-557-4400

San Francisco Arts Commission Gallery 401 Van Ness Ave., 415-554-6080

Absinthe Brasserie and Bar 398 Hayes St., 415-551-1590

route summary

1. Start at United Nations Plaza, at the corner of Market and Leavenworth streets.
2. Walk through U.N. Plaza toward Hyde St.
3. Cross Hyde St. and head west up Fulton St.
4. Turn right at Larkin St., to the Asian Art Museum.
5. Retrace your steps and cross Fulton St. to visit the Main Library.
6. Cross Larkin St. and walk through Civic Center Plaza.
7. Emerge from the plaza and go left on Grove St.
8. Cross Polk St. at Grove St. and enter City Hall through the building's east entrance.
9. Walk through City Hall and exit on the Van Ness Ave. side.
10. Turn right and cross Van Ness Ave. at McAllister St.
11. Turn left (on opposite side of Van Ness Ave.).
12. At Grove St., cross Van Ness Ave. and turn left.
13. At Hyde St. turn right.
14. At Market St. turn left.

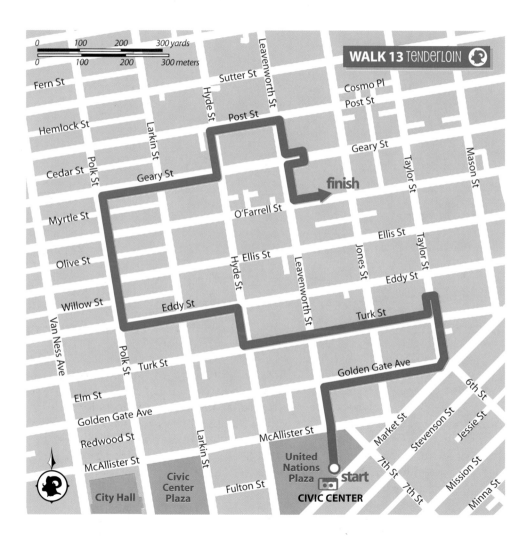

13 TENDERLOIN: EARNING A FINER CUT

BOUNDARIES: **Market St., Taylor St., Post St., Polk St.**
DISTANCE: **Approx. 1 mile**
DIFFICULTY: **Easy**
PARKING: **Street parking is metered, and not necessarily safe. There's a lot next to Original Joe's (corner Taylor and Turk streets) and another at 550 O'Farrell St.**
PUBLIC TRANSIT: **All Market St. Muni buses and streetcars; Civic Center BART**

The Tenderloin, squeezed between Union Square and Civic Center, has long been the part of town where most of the city's low life ends up. It is block after block of Skid Rows lined mostly with residential hotels and rescue missions. Day and night, the sidewalks are crowded with the homeless and the mentally ill as well as a retinue of hustlers and drug dealers. It's all an unpleasant reminder that the American Dream doesn't quite pan out for everybody. That said, the Tenderloin is an incredibly interesting part of town that has intriguing history, good Vietnamese restaurants, great dive bars, and buildings that intimate compelling noir stories—or perhaps their stories are in the Dashiell Hammett vein, for it was here the great crime writer penned his best-loved works. The gay community has had a presence here for decades. Immigrants from Southeast Asia and the Middle East also live and do business in the T.L. Add to the mix a growing number of post-dot-com hipsters who favor the neighborhood's urban grit and the sophisticated night clubs along Geary Ave. and Polk St.

● We'll start from Market St., heading north into the 'Loin on Leavenworth St. On Golden Gate Ave., turn right and you'll spot St. Boniface Roman Catholic Church, built in 1906. Its German Romanesque style is a reflection of the immigrant parishioners of that time. Today St. Boniface, while still quite beautiful, is known more as a daytime refuge for the homeless, dozens of whom snooze in the pews for much of the day. Daily mass, funerals, and even weddings take place in the church to the accompaniment of a quiet chorus of snores. Church staff and the homeless of the T.L. call a nap here "sacred sleep."

● Continue to Taylor St. and turn left. The friendly chef on Original Joe's neon sign is smiling at you, so let's head in that direction. Joe's, which is just across Turk St., has been around since 1937 and retains much of its old-school urban appeal, is the place to go for an honest steak or a 3/4-pound charbroiled burger served on fresh sourdough bread. We mention this because the Tenderloin supposedly derived its name from local cops who were paid higher for walking a tough beat and could afford better cuts of meat. Joe's, meanwhile, is a piece of living history that projects a quietly prideful demeanor. The waiters are all polished professionals in starched shirts who seem to carry on conversations with their regular customers in installments as they circulate between the open grill and their tables. Could be some of these conversations have been going on for years.

- Double back to Turk St. and turn right. We'll pass Aunt Charlies Lounge, at 133 Turk. It's the district's oldest gay bar, and the entertainment here is of the "gender illusionist" and lip-synching variety. The headliner is Gina La Divina, who claims to have spent $65,000 on her breast implants. She's been performing in Frisco since the 1970s.

- Turn right at Hyde St. The parking lot on this corner was the site of the famous Blackhawk nightclub, where in April 1961 Miles Davis' quintet recorded the legendary *Friday and Saturday Night Miles Davis in Person at the Blackhawk, San Francisco.* (It's still available in a four-disc box set.) Next door, an old dive bar called the 222 Club has been rejuvenated. It is now a genuinely hip nightclub that claims a historical connection to the old, long-gone Blackhawk. There's drinking and pizza-eating upstairs, dancing in the basement.

- Hang a left at Eddy and you'll soon spot the Phoenix Hotel, on the corner of Larkin. It's a classic mid-20th century motel, with parking, two levels of rooms, and a kidney-shaped pool—but over the past two decades it's become much more than that. When in San Francisco, rock stars and younger movie stars tend to sleep here. Nirvana, Keanu Reeves, Norah Jones, David Bowie, and countless others have parted the sheets here. The attached Bambuddha Bar is glamour-puss heaven for the see-and-be-seen crowd. It's a genuinely fascinating club, with a groovy, Asian-inspired interior and a huge reclining Buddha on the roof.

- Directly across the street from the Bambuddha, the somewhat drab apartment building at 620 Eddy was the home of author Dashiell Hammett, who lived here with his wife and two daughters from mid-1921 until mid-1926. Hammett was not well known at the time, but he published many of his Continental Op stories, about an unnamed gumshoe, while living here. (We'll see Hammett's next home in just a few blocks.)

● Continue on Eddy to Polk St. and turn right. Here we enter Polk Gulch, world renowned for the gay scene that coalesced here during the 1970s. (Polk St. was the decidedly less-refined flip side of the Castro.) At Olive Alley a huge whale mural comes into view. It tattoos the backside of the Mitchell Brothers O'Farrell Theater, a true landmark in the neighborhood. Along the Polk St. side of the building, an even more eye-catching jungle mural enlivens an entire city block with leopards, tigers, and gorillas lurking in the shadows. Very likely, the mural is meant to suggest the wild sexuality going on within the theater, which can be accessed at 895 O'Farrell St. The theater opened in 1969, and is where Artie and Jim Mitchell screened the low-budget pornographic films they made. The duo gained notoriety with such porn classics as *Behind the Green Door,* starring Marilyn Chambers.

The Mitchell Brothers' empire grew to include 11 theaters throughout California. Apparently, however, trouble was brewing between them. In 1991 Jim shot and killed Artie, copped a manslaughter conviction, and served six years in jail. Nevertheless, the theater, long ago converted into a live strip club, is considered one of the city's classiest venues for exotic dancing. A couple of doors down, the Great American Music Hall is a former bordello that's surprisingly posh inside. It's an excellent live-music venue that books quality touring acts several nights a week.

● Continue on Polk and turn right at Geary St. You might be tempted to stop for a pint of Fullers or a dram of Laphroig at Edinburgh Castle, but let's

O'Farrell Theater marquee

hold that thought for future reference. The huge old pub is worth noting for its cultural contribution to the neighborhood and the city at large. Manager Alan Black, a man with an admirable fondness for working-class literature, has turned the pub's upstairs room into a theater where plays, live music, and readings are performed. Black and his partners also run a publishing house. Irvine Welsh, author of *Trainspotting,* has made several appearances at the pub, where he has read from his work and witnessed a dramatic adaptation of *Trainspotting.* Welsh apparently took a liking to San Francisco, for he moved to the city in 2003.

● Continue on Geary, noting some of the historic old dives, such as the Ha Ra, which opened way back in 1947. The Gangway, a few doors up Larkin St., is an old gay dive bar with an obvious sailor theme—the rickety bow of the *Titanic* juts out from the facade.

● At Hyde St., turn left, then pause at the corner of Post before turning right. The very smart-looking apartment building at 891 Post was home to Hammett from at least late 1927 through the end of 1928. He may have lived here even longer, as a plaque on the side of the building suggests. It is very likely that Hammett wrote *Red Harvest* and *Dain Curse* while living here, and he probably drafted *The Maltese Falcon* in the apartment as well. Literary sleuths like author Don Herron, reading *Falcon* very closely, have deduced that Sam Spade's apartment must have been in this building.

● At the other end of this block, Kayo Books sells old paperback mysteries and sleazy fiction from the '50s and '60s—it's a fun little shop and a true homage to the neighborhood's history and culture.

● Make a right at Leavenworth, then turn left on Geary for a look at the fantastic Alcazar Theater. Built for the Shriners in 1917, and designed by T. Patterson Ross (himself a Shriner), the theater, with its intricate archways clad in ornate tiles, is meant to evoke Byzantine grandeur. You'll notice some familiar motifs—above a second story window on the far right look for a Shriner fez.

● From here, head on down Geary to Union Square, or go around the block for a fine vegetarian Vietnamese meal at Golden Era Vegetarian Restaurant, on O'Farrell St. The food and atmosphere are top notch.

POINTS OF INTEREST

Original Joe's 144 Taylor St., 415-775-4877

Aunt Charlie's Lounge 133 Turk St., 415-441-2922

222 Club 222 Hyde St., 415-440-0222

Phoenix Hotel 601 Eddy St., 415-776-1380

Mitchell Bros. O'Farrell Theater 895 O'Farrell St., 415-776-6686

Great American Music Hall 859 O'Farrell St., 415-885-0750

Edinburgh Castle 950 Geary St., 415-885-4074

Ha Ra 875 Geary St., 415-673-3148

Gangway 841 Larkin St., 415-776-6828

Kayo Books 814 Post St., 415-749-0554

Golden Era Vegetarian Restaurant 572 O'Farrell St., 415-673-3136

route summary

1. Begin at the corner of Market and Leavenworth streets and head north to Golden Gate St. and turn right.
2. Turn left on Taylor St.
3. Cross Turk to Original Joe's; retrace your steps and turn right on Turk St.
4. Turn right on Hyde St.
5. Turn left on Eddy St.
6. Turn right on Polk St.
7. Turn right on Geary St.
8. Turn left on Hyde St.
9. Turn right on Post St.
10. Turn right on Leavenworth St.
11. Turn left on Geary St.

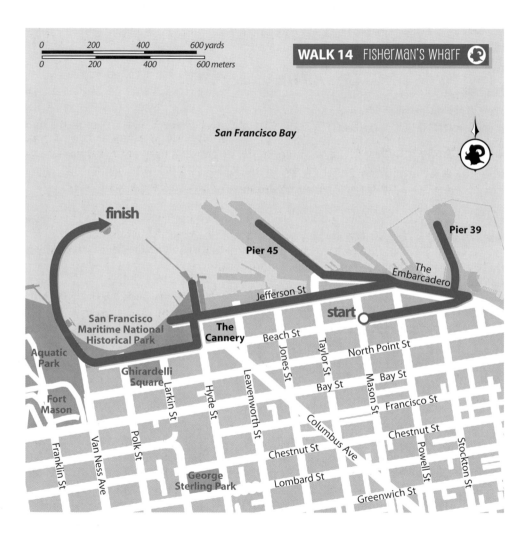

0   200   400   600 yards
0   200   400   600 meters

San Francisco Bay

finish

Pier 39

Pier 45

The Embarcadero

Jefferson St

start

San Francisco Maritime National Historical Park

The Cannery

Beach St

Jones St

Taylor St

North Point St

Aquatic Park

Ghirardelli Square

Larkin St

Hyde St

Leavenworth St

Bay St

Mason St

Bay St

Fort Mason

Francisco St

Polk St

Columbus Ave

Chestnut St

Powell St

Stockton St

Franklin St

Van Ness Ave

George Sterling Park

Chestnut St

Lombard St

Greenwich St

14 FISHERMAN'S WHARF: WHEN IN ROME, DO AS THE TOURIST FROM YPSILANTI, MICHIGAN, DOES

BOUNDARIES: **Beach St., Jefferson St., Grant Ave., Aquatic Park**
DISTANCE: **2½ miles**
DIFFICULTY: **Easy**
PARKING: **Off-street parking is available at the Anchorage Square Garage, corner of Leavenworth and Beach streets. Most street parking is metered seven days a week. On side streets south of Bay St. you might find unmetered street parking, limited to two hours for non-residents (on Sunday you can park for an unlimited time in these zones).**
PUBLIC TRANSIT: **F streetcar; Powell-Mason cable car; 30 and 42 Muni buses**

Nothing against tourists from Ypsilanti, mind you. But Fisherman's Wharf is the prototypical tourist trap, and for that reason most San Franciscans regard the neighborhood as a party that they haven't been invited to, and that they wouldn't want to attend anyway. But to go on deliberately avoiding this cash cow of a neighborhood is to lack curiosity.

For the most part the attractions here fail to reward an ironic approach, although, for some, it helps to be cloaked in such armor. A genuine appreciation for the city's maritime history will go much further. Here and there you'll also encounter aged remnants of Fisherman's Wharf's origins as a tourist trap—old boats, seafood stalls, and family-owned restaurants that opened way back in the 1930s. None of this is to suggest that after taking this tour you're likely to make a habit of spending time down here. But after separating wheat from chaff, you're sure to agree the neighborhood yields a surprising bounty.

● Start at the Longshoremen's Hall, a homely but historic structure at the corner of Mason and Beach streets. It houses the headquarters of the International Longshoremen's and Warehousemen's Union. Bodies outlined on the sidewalk suggest this corner was a crime scene, but these figures are tributes to the striking longshoremen who were shot by police during the general strike of 1934. The riot and shootings took place not here, but on the corner of Mission and Steuart streets, where the Coast Seamen's Union kept its offices. A significant historic event did take place in this building in January 1966, when the Trips Festival was held here.

The three-day event, organized by author Ken Kesey (who penned *One Flew Over the Cuckoo's Nest*), rock promoter Bill Graham, and others, ushered in the hippie era. Entertainment was provided by the Grateful Dead, Big Brother and the Holding Company, light shows, and a "stroboscopic trampolinist" who hopped up and down with a ski mask on while a strobe light flickered on him. The real point of the festival was to drop acid, and some 6,000 people showed up to turn on. Take a look through the plate glass windows and imagine the place full of wigged-out hippies.

● Go east (right) onto Beach St., which hits Jefferson St. Cross Jefferson to enter Pier 39. This open-air shopping center is about as touristy as it gets. It's a midway of shops that obviously prey upon impulsive shoppers. Head straight to the San Francisco Carousel, a handcrafted classic made in Italy. Horses and chariots rotate around a mechanical organ in the center. Rides cost $3. Also pay a visit to K Dock, at the pier's western side, where a small colony of California sea lions overtook a row of boat docks in 1990. The colony quickly grew, and now as many as 900 barking sea lions compete for space on the docks on a winter's day. In summer, most of them migrate to warmer waters to breed, but a few usually haul out here year-round. They're rightly the biggest attraction on Pier 39.

● Exiting the Pier, turn right onto Jefferson St. and walk two blocks until you see and smell the Boudin Bakery. The modern building is nothing much to look at, but the company has been providing the city with sourdough bread since 1849, and some of its "mother dough" is said to have been carried over from the first batch. No need to stop, unless you want a snack.

● Veer right, onto Pier 45. The sight of a submarine and a liberty ship from World War II will tell you you're on the right track. The submarine is the USS *Pampanito,* which patrolled the Pacific during the latter half of the war. You can board the sub to see how uncomfortable life beneath the waves must have been, and to puzzle over the state-of-the art technology of a bygone era. The liberty ship is the SS *Jeremiah O'Brien,* a cargo-carrying vessel that delivered supplies to Normandy on D-Day. It's fully outfitted and in working order. Board and head straight for the engine room for an astonishing view of the ship's awesome 2,700-horsepower, triple-expansion steam engine. *Steamboy* fans will be in heaven.

- Also on Pier 45, the Musée Mécanique is the hidden gem of Fisherman's Wharf. For some, it's the only excuse to venture into this part of town. It's the private collection of Edward Galland Zelinsky, consisting of mechanical amusements and games, mostly from the early 20th century. Risqué mutoscope moving pictures (mostly of women showing their ankles), player pianos, and old-fashioned black-and-white photo booths will easily suck the quarters out of your pockets. Save a few coins for the real showstoppers—"automata" displays of carnivals and circuses, toothpick Ferris wheels, and even a Chinese opium den with a dragon that peeps out from behind a curtain. Be sure to pump some quarters into Laffin' Sal to keep her howling. Her belly laughs are infectious. Some of the one-of-a-kind machines here are fine works of folk art.

- About an hour later, as you reemerge into the real world, head directly back toward Jefferson St. On the way you'll pass the oldest seafood restaurants in the district. Fishermen's Grotto No. 9 was the postcard establishment of the local tourism industry about half a century ago. It opened in 1935 and is still owned by the Geraldi family. Inside you'll find a swanky mid-century bar that's not always open. There's also a gift shop that includes some dusty old relics that have probably sat on the shelves for several decades. Most of the seafood restaurants on the wharf are named for Italian families, reflecting the traditional dominance of Italian fishermen in the local seafood industry. The families of fishermen often ran little seafood stalls to augment their income, and these eventually became restaurants. Most of the restaurants still operate sidewalk stalls selling boiled crab and clam

An iconic Fisherman's Wharf restaurant

chowder served up in hollowed-out loaves of sourdough bread. These are your best bet if you're hungry.

- Turn right at Jefferson. Behind Fishermen's Grotto some very charming and collectible leisure craft—wooden two-seaters mostly—are moored. A block down, at Jefferson and Leavenworth, is the Cannery, an old Del Monte plant that was converted into a shopping center in 1968. The old brick plant was built in 1907 for the Fruit Packers Association, which packed fruit and produce grown in the Central Valley. A courtyard that separates the Cannery from the brick Haslett Warehouse is a nice space where a few restaurants and a bar have tables on the patio, and musicians perform around lunchtime. Jack's Cannery serves decent pub grub here.

- In the Haslett Warehouse, on the corner of Jefferson and Hyde, the Maritime Visitor Center is a gateway to the shipping history that more or less takes over this tour. There's a beautiful antique lighthouse glass set up in front, affording a rare up-close look. The bulk of the space here is dedicated to generally excellent exhibits of art and archival material that tell the story of the seafarers and explorers who passed through the Golden Gate. Entry is free. Upstairs, the Haslett Warehouse has been converted into the boutique Argonaut Hotel.

- Across Jefferson, the entry to Hyde St. Pier is obvious, thanks to a large sign spanning the pier. You'll also quickly spot the fleet of 19th century ships tied up here. These include the *Balclutha,* a square-rigger that regularly traveled the route around Cape Horn from San Francisco to Europe; the *Alma,* a graceful flat-bottomed scow that transported grain to communities around San Francisco Bay; and the *C.A. Thayer,* a three-masted schooner that carried lumber up and down the Pacific Coast. There are many more vessels and items of interest here, and visitors are free to casually explore them. The pier itself was a ferry launch for Route 101 automobile traffic until the Golden Gate Bridge was completed in 1937. Admission is $5.

- The Hyde St. Pier flanks one side of Aquatic Park, a small park that slopes down to a narrow crescent of sand. A sidewalk leads from the pier round the beach, where you'll spot hearty swimmers braving the icy cold waters of the bay.

- Rather than round the beach, though, cut straight out on Hyde St. (We'll make our way back to the water in a few minutes.) The Buena Vista Cafe, at the corner of Hyde and Beach, overlooks the park. It's one of San Francisco's classic saloons, having opened in 1916 in an old boarding house. The place stakes its reputation on having introduced Irish coffee to the U.S. in 1952, and there's usually a row of glasses lined up on the bar awaiting hot coffee, a jigger of Irish whiskey, and a dollop of whipped cream. On a clammy San Francisco day, it's what the doctor ordered.

- Turn right on Beach St. and you'll soon reach Ghirardelli Square, where the Ghirardelli Chocolate Co. moved to from its former location in Jackson Square (see Walk No. 6, the Jackson Square walk). The red brick Chocolate Building was completed in 1899, and as the company grew, founder Domingo Ghirardelli's sons added the Cocoa Building (1900), the Clock Tower (1911), and the Power House (1915). The huge sign atop the complex is one of San Francisco's most recognizable landmarks. The company moved its operations to the East Bay in the early 1960s, and the complex reopened as a shopping center in 1964.

- At the corner of Beach and Polk streets, overlooking Aquatic Park, is the San Francisco National Maritime Museum. It is appropriately housed in the art deco Sala Burton Building shaped like a steamship, replete with portholes. It was a public bath house and a casino before being repurposed for the Maritime Museum. The museum is currently closed for restoration. Should it be open again by the time you read this, be sure to enter the lobby to see Hilaire Hiler's whimsical floor-to-ceiling mural depicting a trippy underwater scene. There are some interesting sculptures by Beniamino Bufano and an abstract mosaic work by Sargent Johnson on the veranda. If the museum is closed, you can still admire Johnson's green slate carvings around the front entrance.

- From the Maritime Museum, make your way back toward the beach, and turn left onto the walkway, which will lead to the eyelash-shaped Municipal Pier, which gets you out into the bay without a boat.

POINTS OF INTEREST

Boudin Bakery 160 Jefferson St., 415-928-1849

USS *Pampanito* Pier 45, 415-561-7006

SS *Jeremiah O'Brien* Pier 45, 415-544-0100

Fisherman's Grotto No 9 Fisherman's Wharf, 415-673-7025

Maritime Visitor Center Hyde and Jefferson streets, 415-447-5000

Argonaut Hotel 495 Jefferson St., 415-563-0800

Hyde St. Pier 415-447-5000

Buena Vista Cafe 2765 Hyde St., 415-474-5044

San Francisco National Maritime Museum 900 Beach St., 415- 561-7100

ROUTE SUMMARY

1. Start at the corner of Mason and Beach streets.
2. Head three blocks east (right) on Beach St. and turn left onto Jefferson St.
3. Cross Jefferson St. and enter Pier 39.
4. Go to the San Francisco Carousel, and then to K Dock to see the sea lions before exiting back onto Jefferson St.
5. Turn right and follow Jefferson St. 2½ blocks and turn right onto Pier 45.
6. Exit Pier 45 and walk past the Fisherman's Grotto No. 9 back to Jefferson St.
7. Turn right and follow Jefferson St. two blocks to the Cannery.
8. Cross Jefferson St. to enter Hyde St. Pier.
9. Exit Hyde St. Pier and cut over to the corner of Hyde and Beach streets and turn right on Beach St.
10. Past the Maritime Museum, at Polk St., turn right to sidewalk that follows the curve of the beach.
11. Follow the curve onto the Municipal Pier and walk all the way to the pier's end.

The Balclutha

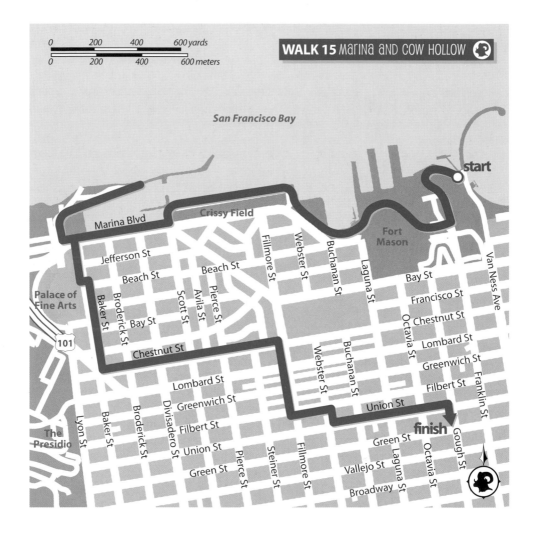

0 200 400 600 yards
0 200 400 600 meters

WALK 15 Marina and Cow Hollow

San Francisco Bay

start

Marina Blvd
Crissy Field
Fort Mason

Jefferson St
Beach St
Beach St
Fillmore St
Webster St
Buchanan St
Laguna St
Bay St
Van Ness Ave

Palace of
Fine Arts
Baker St
Broderick St
Scott St
Avila St
Pierce St
Bay St
Francisco St
Octavia St
Chestnut St

101
Chestnut St
Webster St
Buchanan St
Lombard St
Greenwich St
Franklin St

Lombard St
Filbert St

The
Presidio
Lyon St
Baker St
Broderick St
Divisadero St
Greenwich St
Filbert St
Union St
Green St
Webster St
Union St
Green St
Pierce St
Steiner St
Fillmore St
Green St
Vallejo St
Laguna St
Octavia St
Gough St
finish
Broadway

15 Marina and Cow Hollow: Swinging in the Urban Jungle Gym with Well-to-Do Youngsters

BOUNDARIES: **Van Ness Ave., Baker St., Green St., and San Francisco Bay.**
DISTANCE: **3½ miles**
DIFFICULTY: **Easy**
PARKING: **Off-street parking in Fisherman's Wharf is your best bet.**
PUBLIC TRANSIT: **Powell-Hyde cable car; 30, 42, 47 Muni buses**

The Marina might be summed up as the new-money counterpart to old-money Pacific Heights. Both are upper-class enclaves, but while Pacific Heights rises above the city with a Victorian regalness, the Marina thrusts its chest out into the bay with a 20th century brashness. Cow Hollow, being neither up the hill nor along the bay, more or less slides into the Marina, and the two neighborhoods feel like two parts of a whole. Single professionals have been drawn to the area since the yuppies of the 1980s claimed the neighborhood. You'll encounter young urban professionals throughout the city, but those of the Marina and Cow Hollow still seem to be of their own special type. The districts are remarkably mainstream, at least by San Francisco standards. The city's countercultural leanings are little felt here. On this walk, we'll set out to appreciate the Marina's location with a brisk hike along the bayfront, then loop back down the commercial Main Streets of both neighborhoods.

● Start at Aquatic Park, just beyond the end of Van Ness Ave., where a paved footpath follows the curve of a rare bayside beach. Follow the path toward (but not onto) the eyelash-shaped pier, then go left on McDowell Rd. and follow the ramp up to Fort Mason. (The Fort Mason GGNRA sign will tell you you're on the right track.) At Bunker Rd., behind the Youth Hostel, double back up the two-track dirt road, which leads to the 1863 Battery. If you're one who trembles at the thought of a Confederate invasion of San Francisco Bay, then you'll feel safe in this shady spot armed with a Civil War–era cannon. So far, the cannon has never been fired in hostility. Let's hope it stays that way. This promontory became a defensive battery way back in 1797, when the Spanish established the Battery San Jose here.

- Follow the trail past the cannon and some picnic tables, and then go up some concrete steps. At the top of the steps, a concrete path leads into the residential part of Fort Mason. The fine Victorians along the east side of Franklin St. were originally built for civilians. Although the land was always owned by the military, as the city grew quickly in the 1850s developers went ahead and built homes here, in what was then known as Black Point. It was a gamble worth taking, for the front row views of the bay from the bluffs here are spectacular. Eventually, these homes housed military officers. The last building on the left, at the corner of Pope St. and MacArthur Ave., is the Officers' Club.

- Nothing against officers, but head in the opposite direction. You'll soon reach the Visitor Center, where you can grab maps and literature for future visits to the Golden Gate National Recreation Area, of which Fort Mason is a part. Past it, look for the blacktop path the wends through the green of the Great Meadow. In one corner, before a grassy amphitheater, a statue of the late Congressman Phillip Burton appears to be orating. Burton chaired a subcommittee on national parks and increased the amount of protected parkland in the United States during the late 1970s.

- Follow the path through the Great Meadow until tile roofs to the northwest come into view. Head in that direction and you'll find a sign that says "piers," with an arrow pointing down. That's the idea. You'll see the steps, which lead to the lower half of Fort Mason. Three piers and five whitewashed wooden warehouses remain from what was the U.S.'s largest embarkation port on the Pacific from the time of the Spanish American War on through to World War II. These piers and sheds were built by 1915. During the 1960s, as the military began shutting the fort down, Congressman Burton set his sights on creating a national park, the GGNRA, to include these scenic bluffs and historic buildings. The sheds today house an assortment of cultural institutions, including the renowned Magic Theatre, which has premiered works by Sam Shepard and David Mamet among others. Also here is Greens, one of the more famous vegetarian restaurants in the country. Affiliated with the Zen Center of San Francisco, Greens opened in 1979. If it's mealtime, you can grab a healthy sack lunch and find a spot on the piers for a picnic. Also while here, take a look inside SFMoMA's Artists' Gallery, where works by contemporary artists are exhibited, rented, and sold. Then duck into Book Bay Fort Mason, where the Friends of the San Francisco Public Library sell off the SFPL's cast-off books and movies at bargain prices.

- From Fort Mason, an asphalt path rounds a small yacht harbor before meeting the sidewalks of the Marina Green, a long, gusty lawn along the bayshore that's perfect for kite flying. As the flatness of the terrain here makes apparent, much of the Marina is landfill, created shortly before and directly after the 1906 quake. Some of the fill is said to be rubble from buildings toppled during the quake, which is ironic, considering buildings on landfill are particularly vulnerable during earthquakes. Liquefaction occurs as the earth beneath the streets is shaken, turning the ground beneath foundations into jelly. This phenomenon was borne out alarmingly during the 1989 Loma Prieta earthquake, which inflicted more damage on the Marina than on any other part of the city.

- The Marina Green is a long, uneventful stretch, so just enjoy the view and the exercise. The sailing craft moored in the harbor here belong to members of the exclusive St. Francis Yacht Club, founded in 1927, and the Golden Gate Yacht Club, founded 12 years later. The landfill and the harbor here were completed in time for the 1915 Panama Pacific Exhibition, which ostensibly celebrated the opening of the Panama Canal. Of course, the fair also demonstrated the reemergence of San Francisco, just nine years after the city had been laid to waste, and it promoted the new patch of real estate that would soon become the Marina District. Strange and exotic buildings covered much of the fairgrounds, only to be torn down immediately afterwards. The Mediterranean style housing you see here now mostly went up in the 1920s.

- The Marina Green sidles up to Marina Blvd. for several blocks. At Baker St. turn right and then right again onto Yacht Rd. Follow the road

Fort Mason housing

109

all the way to the end to reach the Wave Organ, and unusual example of environmental art. Built by Peter Richards and George Gonzales in 1986, the Wave Organ is constructed of PVC pipe and busted headstones salvaged from a dismantled graveyard. The idea is to appreciate the sounds created by the tides passing through the pipes. Press an ear against the listening tubes that poke up out of the cobblestones—each one sounds different. The rumbling tones have a profound hush, like an amplified seashell. There's even a stereo booth, where various sounds come at you from several tubes. The Wave Organ sounds best during high tide, which sometimes occurs at an unaccommodating time of day. (Check the website www.saltwatertides.com to see a tidal timetable for the day of your walk.) At lower tides, the sound emanating from the tubes resembles the chugging and wheezing of an old toilet. Still, it's unusual enough to warrant an out-of-the-way side trip.

● Return to Marina Blvd. and turn left on Baker St. A block up, the stately pillars of Bernard Maybeck's Palace of Fine Arts reflect off a duck pond. The palace, designed to look like a gutted classical ruin, is the only architectural showpiece spared after the Panama Pacific Exhibition. The original, made of plaster and chicken wire, wasn't designed to last, but it was faithfully rebuilt of durable concrete in the 1960s. Behind it, a shed from the fair also survives and houses the Exploratorium, a fun science museum.

● Stay on Baker until you reach Chestnut St., where a left turn leads into a fashionable shopping strip. Here, it may suddenly dawn on you that the Marina is the Beverly Hills of San Francisco, where everyone looks like a celebrity and some actually are. Among the expensive clothiers and fitness centers are a handful of spots to grab a cup of coffee or a bite to eat. Bechelli's is a classic coffee shop with swivel stools around a horseshoe counter. It has that traditional Main Street feel and the basic menu you'd expect in such a place. A few blocks up, Lucca Delicatessen has all the hallmarks of a great Italian deli, with the aroma of salamis and cheeses wafting out to the sidewalk, luring you in. There's a park ahead, if you want to grab a sandwich to go.

● At Fillmore St. turn right. After crossing busy Lombard St. you enter Cow Hollow. A block down, the Balboa Cafe welcomes you to the neighborhood. It's a great old bar and grill, open since 1913, with an interior that would look right at home in an Edward Hopper painting. Over lunch, you can enjoy the place for its historic atmosphere, but at night the neighborhood's noisy singles scene engulfs it. It was on the yuppie socialite map during the 1980s and remains hot today. Mayor Gavin Newsom, himself more a young urban entrepreneur (a "yueie"?), once owned it.

● Turn left on Filbert St. At the corner of Webster St., where you turn right, the **Vedanta Temple** is one of the most exotic-looking places of worship in San Francisco. The Victorian pile is a purple flight of fancy with Moorish arches and turrets. It was built in 1905 by the Swami Trigunatitananda, the Hindu monk who founded the Vedanta Society of Northern California. Every tower is different—notice the medieval battlement atop one. Turn the corner to admire it from all sides.

● A block down Webster make a left on Union St., the main drag. Union is, you might say, visually busier than Chestnut St., with tighter clothes, bigger hairstyles, and bars that attract singles. Perry's, at No. 1944, has the feel of an old New York tavern, and indeed the bar was moved here from the Upper East Side in 1969. Most of the time it's a casual neighborhood joint where you can watch a few innings of baseball over a beer and a burger. Late at night, though, Perry's is the archetypical "breeder" bar.

● Turn right on Gough St. for a look at the Colonial Dames Octagon House, at No. 2645. It was built in 1861. See the Russian Hill tour for background on unusual eight-sided houses such as this one. Next to it is a wooded park surrounded by an unpainted picket fence—a good spot to get off your feet after a long walk. Van Ness Ave. is just two blocks away.

POINTS OF INTEREST

Greens Fort Mason Center, Building A, 415-771-6222

Book Bay Fort Mason, Fort Mason Center, Building C, 415-771-1076

Exploratorium 3601 Lyon St., 415-563-7337

Bechelli's 2346 Chestnut St., 415-346-1801

Balboa Cafe 3199 Fillmore St., 415-921-3944

Vedanta Temple 2963 Webster St.

Perry's 1944 Union St., 415-922-9022

Colonial Dames Octagon House 2645 Gough St., 415-441-7512

route summary

1. Start at the northern end of Van Ness Ave., and follow the path left, in a northwesterly direction around Aquatic Park.

2. Before you reach the pier, turn left on McDowell Ave.

3. Follow the path up the hill into Fort Mason.

4. Behind the Youth Hostel, turn left onto the two-track dirt road.

5. Past the cannon and picnic tables, follow steps up. A path will lead from the top of the steps to Pope St. residences.

6. Turn right on MacArthur Ave.

7. At the Great Meadow, follow the curving path to the right.

8. At the northern side of the meadow, look for the sign that says "piers," pointing down steps that lead to the piers and warehouses of Fort Mason Center.

9. Past Fort Mason Center, turn right onto asphalt path that hems the boat harbor.

10. Follow the sidewalk west, through the Marina Green.

11. Turn right at Baker St.

12. Turn right at Yacht Rd. and follow it to the Wave Organ, at the end.

13. Return to Baker St. and bear left, heading south.

14. Turn left on Chestnut St.

15. Turn right on Fillmore St.

16. Turn left on Filbert St.

17. Turn right on Webster St.

18. Turn left on Union St.

19. Turn right on Gough St.

Vedanta Temple

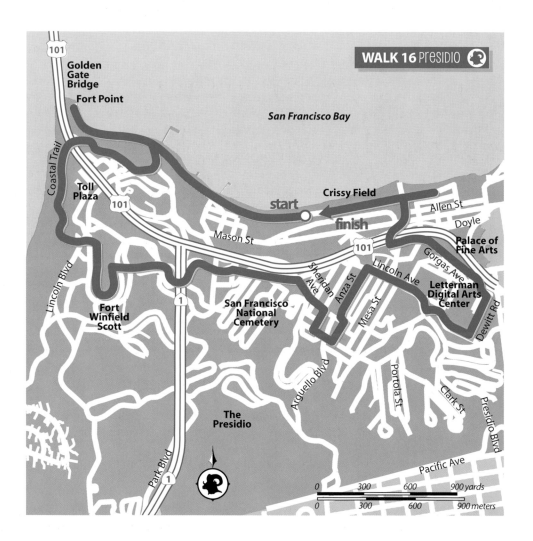

101

Golden Gate Bridge

Fort Point

San Francisco Bay

Coastal Trail

Toll Plaza

101

start

Crissy Field

Allen St

Doyle

finish

Mason St

101

Palace of Fine Arts

Gorgas Ave

Sheridan Ave

Anza St

Lincoln Ave

Letterman Digital Arts Center

Lincoln Blvd

1

Fort Winfield Scott

San Francisco National Cemetery

Mesa St

Dewitt Rd

Arguello Blvd

Portola St

Clark St

Presidio Blvd

The Presidio

Park Blvd

1

Pacific Ave

| 0 | 300 | 600 | 900 yards |
| 0 | 300 | 600 | 900 meters |

16 Presidio: Baywatching and Invading Old Forts

BOUNDARIES: Crissy Field, Golden Gate Bridge, Letterman Complex
DISTANCE: 5½ miles
DIFFICULTY: Moderate (but long)
PARKING: Free parking is available in several lots along Crissy Field.
PUBLIC TRANSIT: The 30 Muni bus terminates on Broderick St., a block outside the park, near Crissy Field.

The Presidio, along with Mission Dolores, was just about all there was to San Francisco during the city's Spanish period. It was the military post, linked to the mission via a trail that later became Divisadero St. Its location overlooking the Golden Gate was suitable for guarding the entrance to San Francisco Bay. The Presidio's 1,000 acres remained a military post under the Mexican government. Under U.S. rule, the Presidio was an Army base until 1994, when it was turned over to the National Park System. As a park, it has a lot to offer. Its historic buildings include one of the city's very oldest structures, as well as many buildings from the Civil War period. Some rows of military housing built in the Colonial Revival style resemble a Norman Rockwell vision of small-town America, fronted by wide porches and showing plenty of red brick and white trim. San Francisco's most recognizable architectural feature, the Golden Gate Bridge, touches down on the park's northern tip. Meanwhile, post-military tenants of the park include George Lucas, whose film-production companies are based here. But it's the land and the location that make the Presidio special, for during its two centuries as a military base the area was spared the rapid development that went on outside its walls. Thus, an extraordinary swath of nature has been preserved for the leisurely enjoyment of the modern civilian. It is a huge and varied parkland, with cliffside trails overlooking the Pacific Ocean and a long, low-lying bayshore that draws walkers and bikers in great numbers. This tour is lengthy (over 5 miles), but doesn't even cover half the park. Regard it as an introduction to the key sights, and come back to explore the park further on your own.

● **Start at Crissy Field, where San Franciscans come to appreciate their bay, and walk in the direction of the Golden Gate Bridge. The level grassy strip to the left was an airfield, formed by the Army in 1919. These were fairly early days in the development** of flight, and many landmark voyages took off or landed here, including test runs at transcontinental flights. (Then, it took three days to fly from here to New York—about as long as a cross-country trip by Greyhound bus today—with numerous pit stops along the way.) In 1924, the first round-the-world journey by air made a heroic stop at Crissy Field before concluding at its starting point in Seattle, Washington. Two of the four aircraft that began the journey made it to the finish. The other two crashed. It was a dangerous endeavor for the times. The runway is said to be intact, but only kites and Frisbees take off here these days.

- Along the cinder path you'll see marshlands that are being restored to their pre-Army state. Already the marshes attract plenty of migrating birds, including the great blue heron, whose elegant flight surely puts human flying machines to shame.

- Just beyond Crissy Field is the Warming Hut, a welcoming gift shop and snack stand that serves up hot beverages and high-quality sandwiches made with local and organic ingredients.

- Continue along the bayfront sidewalk to Fort Point, with the Golden Gate Bridge arching dramatically overhead. Along the way, take note of steps heading uphill to the left (we'll walk up there in a bit). Also check out the stone embankment, where Kim Novak took her dip into the bay in Hitchcock's *Vertigo*. (She was fully clothed, and James Stewart leapt in after her, took her to his apartment, and managed to get her into a bathrobe without violating the strict film code.) On some days you'll see surfers riding the waves just off the point. Fort Point itself, a huge brick and granite fortress, was built in 1853 to protect the entrance to the bay. Construction continued through the Civil War, when it was thought a Confederate attack might arrive by sea. Many other buildings rose in the Presidio during that time, as San Francisco's importance became clear to the vulnerable Union. The perspective of the Golden Gate Bridge—from underneath it—will knock your socks off. The graceful immensity of the bridge fully registers here.

- Backtrack toward the Warming Hut and follow those steps we passed earlier. Towards the top, bear right on the trail that leads to Battery East. Built in 1876, this armed lookout is one of many built in the latter half of the 19th century along the bluffs overlooking the Pacific. Continue on the trail, which passes beneath the bridge toll plaza and by a few more historic batteries before reaching a coastal overlook (just beyond Battery Godfrey). From the overlook, follow Langdon Ct., which loops to Lincoln Blvd., and cross over to Fort Winfield Scott. This complex, built in 1910, has many Mission Revival structures that are fairly consistent with California architecture from the time (as opposed to the Presidio's Colonial Revival structures, which are anomalous in the region).

- Make your way through Fort Winfield Scott and follow Ruckman Ave. past some housing. Bear left onto Rod Rd., toward the Hwy. 1 overpass, walk beneath the pass, and turn left on wide Lincoln Blvd. A little ways down, beyond the stables where equestrian park rangers are based, turn right on Cowles St. Turn left on McDowell Ave.

- Just beneath elevated Doyle Dr.—recognizable by its orange rails that reflect the style of the Golden Gate Bridge (which Doyle feeds into)—pay a visit to the folksy Pet Cemetery, where lie the remains of distinguished critters named "Skippy," "Knucklehead," and "Peep, Pet Pigeon of Johnnie Burke." Take a look around. It's by turns touching, humorous, and overblown.

- Across from the Pet Cemetery, turn right on Crissy Field Ave., which follows the shadow of Doyle Dr. to meandering Lincoln Blvd., which sweeps past the military cemetery on its way to the Main Post and Parade Ground. Bear right on Lincoln to Sheridan Ave. This is a shortcut to the southern end of the Parade Ground, so turn right on it. The grounds have been converted into a parking lot, which adds convenience but detracts from the beauty of the surrounding buildings. Turn right on Montgomery St.,

The Warming Hut at Crissy Field

where the historic Colonial Revival structures, uniform in design, were once barracks housing for enlisted men.

● Turn left on Moraga Ave. and you'll reach the Officers' Club, which still has some adobe walls from the original commandant's headquarters, built in 1776. Other parts of the building were added throughout the 19th and 20th centuries, but go inside and enter the Mesa Lounge (to the left immediately after you enter), where a cut-away reveals some of the old adobe. Note the deep recesses in the walls for the windows—it's a thick old structure. The National Park Service keeps its information center within the Officers' Club, so drop in for maps and books.

● Head back along the east side of the Parade Ground, to Lincoln Blvd. and turn right. Bear left on Letterman Rd. and follow it down to the Letterman Digital Arts Center, where many branches of George Lucas' multimedia empire, including Industrial Light and Magic (Lucas' Oscar-winning special-effects company), are based. Walk around Building B, where (to borrow a familiar dyslexic patois) a fountain presided over by a statue of Yoda is. After admiring the Yoda Fountain, walk between the buildings into the complex's park-like grounds. The grounds are certainly interesting, but are far too carefully landscaped, with perfectly shaped mounds carpeted with an impeccable lawn. An artificial stream trickles down to a "lagoon." Walk through or around the gardens, depending on how enchanted you are, and head out via Gorgas Ave., where you turn left. Turn right on Halleck St., pass back under Doyle Dr., and cross over to Crissy Field. From here it's just about 100 yards back to where you started.

POINTS OF INTEREST

Warming Hut Crissy Field
NPS Visitors Center Officers' Club, 415-561-4323

route summary

1. Start at the Crissy Field parking lot and follow the cinder trail toward the Golden Gate Bridge, all the way to the Warming Hut.
2. Past the Warming Hut walk on the sidewalk along the bay to Fort Point.
3. From Fort Point, backtrack toward the Warming Hut, looking for a trail that heads uphill, across from the Warming Hut.
4. Follow the trail up to Battery East and beneath the bridge toll plaza all the way to the coastal overlook.
5. From the coastal overlook head inland, along Landon Ct.
6. Cross Lincoln Blvd. to Fort Winfield Scott.
7. Pass through Fort Winfield Scott and look for Ruckman Ave. on the other side.
8. Follow Ruckman Ave. to Rod Rd.; go to Lincoln Blvd. and turn left.
9. Turn right on Cowles St.
10. Turn left on McDowell Ave.
11. Across from the Pet Cemetery, turn right on Crissy Field Ave.
12. Bear right onto Lincoln Blvd.
13. Turn right onto Sheridan Ave.
14. At the Parade Ground turn right on Montgomery St.
15. Turn left on Moraga Ave.
16. Turn left on Graham St.
17. Turn right on Lincoln Blvd.
18. Bear left on Letterman Dr.
19. Enter the Letterman Digital Arts Center through the passage next to Building B (past the Yoda Fountain).
20. Past the grounds and "lagoon" of the Letterman Complex, turn left on Gorgas Ave.
21. Turn right on Halleck St. and walk beneath elevated Doyle Dr. back to Crissy Field.

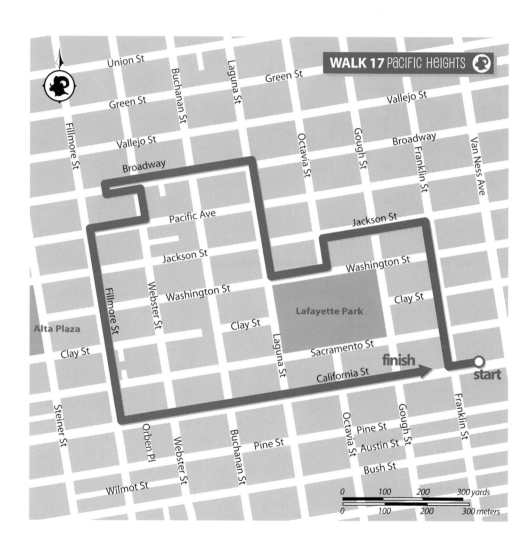

Union St

Green St

Laguna St

Green St

Vallejo St

Buchanan St

Fillmore St

Green St

Vallejo St

Octavia St

Gough St

Broadway

Franklin St

Van Ness Ave

Broadway

Pacific Ave

Jackson St

Jackson St

Washington St

Fillmore St

Webster St

Washington St

Lafayette Park

Clay St

Alta Plaza

Clay St

Clay St

Laguna St

Sacramento St

finish

start

California St

Steiner St

Orben Pl

Webster St

Buchanan St

Pine St

Octavia St

Pine St

Gough St

Franklin St

Austin St

Bush St

Wilmot St

0   100   200   300 yards
0   100   200   300 meters

17 Pacific Heights: Victorian Splendor

BOUNDARIES: **California St., Franklin St., Broadway, Fillmore St.**
DISTANCE: **2 miles**
DIFFICULTY: **Moderately Strenuous**
PARKING: **Off-street parking is available at 1700 California St., just off Van Ness Ave.**
PUBLIC TRANSIT: **1, 42, 47, and 49 Muni buses; California St. cable car.**

San Francisco's elite moved up to Pacific Heights' lofty, rarified environs back in the 1870s and have never left. Well, the original people have died, but their latter-day ilk remain. It seems Nob Hill wasn't big enough for all of the incredibly wealthy citizens of the Victorian city, and the well-to-do staked their claim to hilltop lots here. The grandest mansions in the Heights were once (and in some cases are still) homes of magnates, tycoons, industrialists, and honchos of the class that also have office towers, parks, and streets named for them. Contemporary millionaires from the film and entertainment industry have joined the club relatively recently. Thus, this tour is largely an appreciation of jaw-dropping architectural phenomena. Interestingly, the neighborhood is densely packed, with front and side yards as rare as in any other part of the city, and many streets are dominated by luxury apartment buildings. On a weekday morning, sightseers will share the sidewalk with dog walkers and stroller-pushing nannies.

● **Start at the corner of Van Ness Ave. and California St.**, historically a key intersection for the neighborhood. Here the California St. cable car line terminates, but in the 1870s this line and several others continued up from the downtown area to the top of Pacific Heights, making the area accessible to residents in pre-automobile days. The lines ran up and down most of the east-west streets of the neighborhood. Van Ness, initially, was a residential street where some of the city's very wealthiest built their mansions. At 125 feet wide, Van Ness is the city's broadest thoroughfare, and must have been a real showstopper. During the 1906 conflagration the street's hoity manses were systematically dynamited to create the firebreak that stopped the flames from climbing farther west. Van Ness was rebuilt as a retail strip, and by the middle of the 20th century was lined with steakhouses and flashy auto showrooms.

- Head one block west on California St. and you'll begin to see what remains of the neighborhood's Victorian grandeur. The mansion at 1701 Franklin St. was built by Edward Coleman, a '49 gold miner who, unlike most, actually struck it rich. It stands on a large corner lot, which is common for Pacific Heights—the biggest houses generally stand on corners, the smaller ones mid-block. Up near the eaves the house is banded by a whimsical ornamental trim, with a recurring motif of laurels and torches. The Franklin St. side has a comely stained-glass window.

- Turn right (north) on Franklin. Another stately corner mansion stands at the intersection of Franklin and Clay streets. Now occupied by the Golden Gate Spiritualist Church, this white, wedding-cake house was built for the Crocker family in 1900. The church meetings that go on inside are much more interesting. Founded in 1924 by Rev. Florence S. Becker, the congregation observes the Spiritualist practice of communing with the dead. Services are conducted by mediums, and among the church's principles, which are stated during each service, is that "the existence and personal identity of the individual continue after the change called death." A little farther, on the same side of Franklin St., actor Nicolas Cage owned the large Victorian at No. 1945 for many years. He painted the house black and kept pet snakes while living here part time.

- On the next block of Franklin St., at No. 2007, the Haas-Lilienthal House cuts an impressive figure. Built in 1886 for William Haas, the austere house is one of the city's finest Victorians and reflects the elegance that once typified the neighborhood. Haas' daughter, Alice Haas Lilienthal, lived in the house until 1972, and it was turned over to the Foundation for San Francisco's Architectural Heritage a year later. It's open for tours several days a week ($8).

- Turn left at Jackson St. and left again at Octavia St. This curved, cobbled block was designed to slow traffic as it passed the immense Spreckels mansion, at the top end of the block. Adolf Spreckels, son of sugar magnate Claus Spreckels, built the grand chateau in 1925. Today, romance novelist Danielle Steele lives in it, and she appears to favor the vital decay aesthetic, for the mansion's exterior is faded and peeling. The house appeared as the nightclub Chez Joey in the 1957 film *Pal Joey,* starring Frank Sinatra.

- Lafayette Park, across from the Spreckels mansion, is little more than an overgrown hilltop with windblown patches of lawn where dogs sniff at each other. The park's leveled peak was the site of Samuel Holladay's mansion during the latter half of the 19th century. Holladay was a prominent citizen—he was a judge who also served on the city council—but there is no record of his ever having purchased the land here. The city regarded him as a well-to-do squatter, and tried to evict him. Holladay knew the ins and outs of the law well enough to evade the city's efforts. He lived here until his death in 1915, and the city demolished the house in 1930.

- Turn right at Washington St., and you'll quickly reach the gates of the Phelan mansion, at No. 2150. It was the home of James Phelan, who served as the city's mayor from 1897 to 1902 and in the U.S. Senate from 1915 to 1921. The Renaissance Revival structure is awkward, with an unusual glassed-in mezzanine over the front entry. The former mayor's greatest architectural legacy is the Phelan Building, on Market St. (see the Lower Market St. walk).

- Turn right at Laguna. A block up, the corner house at 2090 Jackson is the Whittier mansion. Just prior to the U.S.'s entry to World War II, this honey-toned sandstone house was purchased by the Nazi government, which intended to use it as a consulate. Those plans were obviously waylaid by the war.

- Continue on Laguna St. and turn left at Broadway. A block and a half up, the huge house at No. 2120 is one of two Flood mansions on the street. This one, built in 1901, was the home of Jennie Flood. It was built by her brother, James Leary Flood, who was the son of silver king James Clair Flood. Jennie was living in her father's Nob Hill mansion,

Haas-Lilienthal House

which was damaged in the 1906 quake, so she moved here. James Leary Flood left a few years later, after building a new home up the street, at No. 2222, for himself and his wife. The second Flood estate, consisting of a nearly identical pair of massive villas, was completed in 1915. It is now the outrageously posh home of the Sacred Heart School, a Catholic academy.

● Having just passed Webster St., double back and turn right (south). The house at 2550 Webster is the Bourn mansion, a dark brick fortress with fantastic chimneys. It was built in 1896 for William Bowers Bourn, inheritor of the Empire Gold Mine, the richest mine in the state. The house was not Bourn's home—just a luxurious pit stop for entertaining guests while he was in town. Willis Polk was the architect.

● Turn right at Pacific Ave. and turn left onto Fillmore St., the principal commercial street of Pacific Heights. It's lined with clothing boutiques, beauty salons, restaurants, and cafes. Nice places to stop for dinner are Jackson Fillmore, an intimate little Italian spot, and the Elite Cafe, an exquisite old-town noshery offering an oyster bar and a decent Cajun menu.

● Turn left at California St. The corner of California and Webster is dominated by the imposing Temple Sherith Israel, one of the pillars of the city's well-established Jewish community. The congregation dates back to the 1850s, and this awesome temple went up in 1904. It is more spectacular inside than out, with a frescoed inner dome and beautiful stained-glass windows conducting a brilliant spectrum on sunny days. Albert Pissis was the architect.

● Three blocks down, at 1990 California, the Atherton House looks humble, considering the size of the Atherton family's fortune. Faxton Atherton owned a huge estate that spanned the Peninsula south of San Francisco. The exclusive city of Atherton is named for him. After his death, his widow built this house for her frequent social calls to the city. It was built in 1881.

● From the Atherton House, it's just a few blocks back to Van Ness Ave.

POINTS OF INTEREST

Jackson Fillmore 2506 Fillmore St., 415-346-5288
Elite Cafe 2049 Fillmore St., 415-346-8668

route summary

1.   Start at the corner of Van Ness Ave. and California St.
2.   Head west on California St.
3.   Turn right on Franklin St.
4.   Turn left on Jackson St.
5.   Turn left on Octavia St.
6.   Turn right on Washington St.
7.   Turn right on Laguna St.
8.   Turn left on Broadway.
9.   Pass Webster St., then double back and turn south on Webster St.
10.   Turn right on Pacific Ave.
11.   Turn left on Fillmore St.
12.   Turn left on California St.

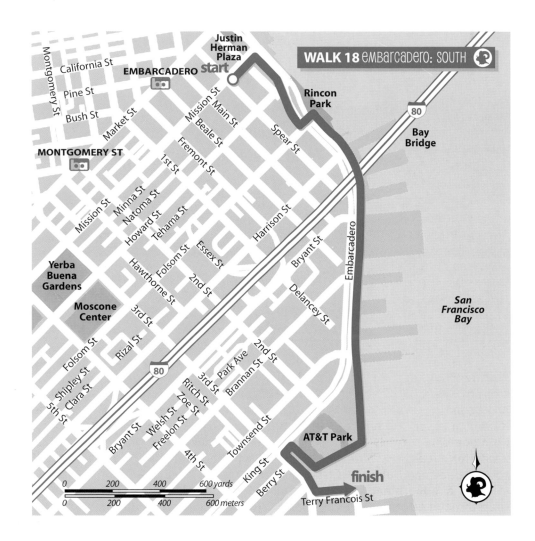

WALK 18 EMBARCADERO: SOUTH

Justin Herman Plaza
EMBARCADERO **start**
Montgomery St
California St
Pine St
Bush St
Market St
MONTGOMERY ST
Mission St
Main St
Mission St
Beale St
Fremont St
1st St
Minna St
Natoma St
Howard St
Tehama St
Folsom St
Essex St
Hawthorne St
2nd St
Yerba Buena Gardens
Moscone Center
3rd St
Rizal St
Folsom St
Shipley St
Clara St
5th St
Bryant St
Welsh St
Zoe St
Freelon St
3rd St
Ritch St
Park Ave
Brannan St
2nd St
4th St
Townsend St
King St
Berry St
Terry Francois St
Spear St
Rincon Park
Harrison St
Bryant St
Delancey St
Embarcadero
80
Bay Bridge
San Francisco Bay
AT&T Park
finish
80

0   200   400   600 yards
0   200   400   600 meters

18 embarcadero (SOUTH): THE DOCKS OF THE BAY AND A BASEBALL BONUS

BOUNDARIES: **Mission St., Spear St., Embarcadero South, King St.**
DISTANCE: **1.75 miles**
DIFFICULTY: **Easy**
PARKING: **There is off-street parking at 50 Howard St. Street parking is all metered and limited to two hours.**
PUBLIC TRANSIT: **F streetcars (street level); J, K, L, M, N, and S streetcars (underground); Embarcadero BART; 1, 2, 7, 14, 21, and 71 Muni buses**

In recent years, no part of San Francisco has changed as much as the waterfront south of Market St. The development of luxury condominiums, high-rise office towers, and the Giants' ballpark has brought new life to an area long ago abandoned by the shipping industry, which moved across the bay to Oakland in the late 1950s. Public art adds color and interest, as do restaurants and bars that tend to get lively before and after baseball games, which is a good time to take this walk. (See the Sporting Green in the *San Francisco Chronicle* for a schedule.) Here and there are remnants of the Embarcadero's long gone stevedore days. On this tour we'll take a close look at the ongoing development of this precious strip of real estate and hopefully catch a few innings of baseball free of charge.

● **Start at the Rincon Annex Post Office, on the corner of Mission and Spear streets. It's no longer functioning as a post office, and as you can see from the street the modern Rincon Center rises up over the building's backside. The historic post office has been preserved in near pristine condition and now serves as a unique foyer to the office tower. The post office is an art deco beauty, dating to 1939. It was saved from demolition in 1978 primarily to protect the murals that grace the interior. Step inside for a look. From 1946 to 1948, Russian-born Anton Refregier painted 27 scenes depicting California history. Some common threads address concerns about freedom of speech and worship, for as Refregier worked on the murals such liberties were threatened in Europe, where Communism was spreading, and also in America, where anti-Communist paranoia had its grip on the country. Refregier's unromanticized scenes are populated by serious, often somber characters. Pass through the** lobby into the newer Rincon Center and you'll reach a large, classy food court, with tables and chairs arranged around a "rain column"—water pours from the ceiling several floors above, expands as it falls, and then appears to collapse neatly as it hits a stone platform on the floor. Your best choice for a light bite here is Yank Sing, one of the best dim sum restaurants in the city.

● A block westward down Mission St., at Steuart St., the Audiffred Building looks like no other San Francisco landmark. It was built in 1889 by Hippolyte d'Audiffred, a French immigrant who in San Francisco sold charcoal to Chinese laundries and parlayed his earnings into real estate. He is believed to have designed this building himself, although he had no training as an architect. Consequently, the Audiffred building is an unusual amalgam of styles: a New England–style brick structure, with Victorian and Gothic details, capped with a mansard roof reminiscent of the Second Empire style popularized in d'Audiffred's native France. The ground floor was originally occupied by the Bulkhead Saloon, where sailors and wharf hands drank, and the Coast Seamen's Union kept offices upstairs. Local legend maintains the building survived the 1906 fires thanks to a wily barkeep, who bribed the fire department with a cart of wine and whiskey. The surrounding buildings all burned to the ground while drunk firemen kept their hoses on the Audiffred Building. During the early 1950s, the upper floors served as artist lofts, and poet Lawrence Ferlinghetti (who also paints) was among the creative souls who rented space here. Today, the ground floor is occupied by Chef Nancy Oakes' excellent Boulevard Restaurant, and its interior design is redolent with Belle Époque details. The restaurant jumps during the weekday lunch hour, when free-spending office workers pour into its swank booths, and its bar is always a lively spot for a classy cocktail.

● Across Mission St. is a monument to the striking longshoremen who were gunned down by police during a demonstration in 1934. It was on this corner that police fired into the crowd, killing Howard Sperry and Nick Bordoise.

● Continue around the Audiffred Building and turn right onto the Embarcadero. No. 250 is headquarters for the Gap company, well-known purveyors of casual clothing. The company was founded in 1969 by Donald and Doris Fisher, who still head the company, which has grown to include more than 3,000 stores. The Gap began by marketing inexpensive blue jeans for teenagers. (The name refers to the 'generation gap.')

Peer through the building's glass doors for a look at Richard Serra's huge metal sculpture, which dominates a five-story atrium. It's called *Charlie Brown,* although it bears no resemblance to Charles M. Schultz's prematurely bald cartoon character.

● Cross the Embarcadero at Folsom St. for an up-close look at *Cupid's Span,* sculptor Coosje van Bruggen's 60-foot high representation of the little cherub's bow and arrow, looking as though it fell from the sky and embedded itself into the ground here.

● Continue walking along this side of the Embarcadero. By now, you're already enjoying a wonderful perspective of the Bay Bridge, which you'll soon be walking under. On the way, at Harrison St., you'll pass the Hills Bros. Coffee Building, with its huge, eye-catching neon sign, and Gordon Biersch, a brewpub. Just as you reach the shadow of the bridge, take note of the fire station at Pier 22½, where two antique fireboats are docked. *Phoenix,* which was built in 1954, was used to pump water out of the bay to douse fires in the Marina after the 1989 earthquake. Afterwards, Marina residents donated funds to purchase *Guardian,* a lovely vessel built in 1951.

● The underbelly of the Bay Bridge is an awesome sight. The size of the bridge, and the effort that went into building it, are difficult to comprehend, especially from this informed vantage point. The bridge hits land at the southern side of Rincon Hill, which in the 1850s and '60s was the city's most fashionable neighborhood. It was here that the first millionaires of the Gold Rush city built their magnificent mansions. There's no sign of the hill's former splendor, as the area declined following development of Nob Hill in the 1870s. After more than a century of neglect, compounded by construction of the

Willie McCovey statue swingin' for McCovey Cove

bridge in the 1930s, new condominiums and offices are going up in this part of town, making Rincon Hill once again a desirable address.

- On down the Embarcadero, at Pier 28, you'll spot an old tavern left from the waterfront's heyday. Called the Hi Dive, it's a smart little joint where you might enjoy a beer and a view of the bay. At Pier 30, in an unprepossessing little shack propped up over the water, is Red's Java House, a classic once patronized by old salts and longshoremen. It still attracts average Joe's today, along with suited office workers. Head on in to this historic joint. In back, toward the loo, the walls are covered with photos by Bruce Steinberg, taken in 1971. These include shots of Red himself, looking every bit the wiry and fierce-tempered grill chef. He doubtless ran an orderly establishment. Red is no longer around, but you can still order a greasy cheeseburger and a cold bottle of Bud for a mere $6.

- Immediately to the south is a dead zone of parking lots where plans are afoot that may not bode well for Red's. The site, extending from Pier 30 to Pier 36, is slated to be redeveloped as a cruise ship terminal, a shopping center, a public park, and a 22-story condominium tower.

- Moseying on down the waterfront, keep your eyes peeled for the historical marker at the far end of Pier 30, which lists the names of 23 men who died while building the Bay Bridge.

- The ballpark begins to exert its gravitational pull here, especially before games, when a stream of pedestrians will be headed in that direction. Approach along the bay, through South Beach Harbor, where sailboats and yachts are docked. Here you'll spot the huge Coke bottle and antique mitt that loom over the center field bleachers. Follow the curve of the stadium, to where the right field arcade overlooks McCovey Cove. Along this side of the ballpark an iron gate permits a view to nonpaying fans, who are allowed to stand here and watch part of a game from the field level, just a few paces beyond the right field warning track. Staff clear the area every three innings to make room for a fresh crowd. Every few months or so one of the ball players launches a titanic home run that plops into McCovey Cove, and it's usually a race between kayakers and dogs to see who can retrieve the ball. Finders keepers is the rule.

● Walking in the same direction around the ballpark leads to a statue of Juan Marichal, the legendary Dominican pitcher whose menacing, high-kick delivery was a beautiful sight to Giants fans. Marichal pitched for the Giants from 1960 to 1973. A little ways farther is Willie Mays Plaza, with a statue of the greatest ball player ever to wear a Giants uniform. Some say he was the best, period. For two decades Mays hit for power, stole bases, and played the outfield with extraordinary ability, intuition, and spirit. Mays began his career with the New York Giants in 1951, coming to San Francisco when the team relocated in 1958.

● At Willie Mays Plaza, turn left onto 3rd St. and cross the Lefty O'Doul Bridge, named for Francis "Lefty" O'Doul, a ballplayer who won the National League batting crown in 1929, with a remarkable .398 average. San Francisco was his hometown. O'Doul managed the San Francisco Seals, of the Pacific Coast League, from 1935 to 1951. The bridge named for him is a charmer, a Strauss trunnion bascule span built in 1933 that crosses narrow Mission Creek.

● Once you've crossed the bridge hook left and walk along McCovey Cove, on the opposite side from the ballpark. This is China Basin Park. You'll reach a statue of Willie McCovey, the slugging first baseman who was known as "Stretch" for his great size and for his ability to reach for wild throws to first. McCovey began his career in 1959 and retired in 1980. Also in the park is a perfect T-ball field, with a pint-sized diamond for pip-squeak ballplayers.

POINTS OF INTEREST

Yank Sing 101 Spear St., 415-957-9300

Boulevard Restaurant Mission St., 415-543-6084

Hi Dive Pier 28-1/2, 415-977-0170

Red's Java House Pier 30, 415-777-5626

AT&T Park 24 Willie Mays Plaza (corner 3rd and King streets), 415-972-1800

route summary

1. Start at Rincon Center (the former U.S. Post Office), corner of Mission and Spear streets.

2. Walk west down Mission St. toward the bay.

3. Turn right onto the Embarcadero.

4. Walk down to Folsom St. and turn left to cross the Embarcadero.

5. Continue down Embarcadero, beneath and then past the Bay Bridge.

6. Follow walkway along the bayfront as it veers away from the street, along South Beach Harbor.

7. Continue to the ballpark, then around it, along McCovey Cove.

8. At Willie Mays Plaza, on 3rd St., turn left and cross Lefty O'Doul Bridge.

9. On the other side of the bridge, turn left into China Basin Park.

Cupid's Span

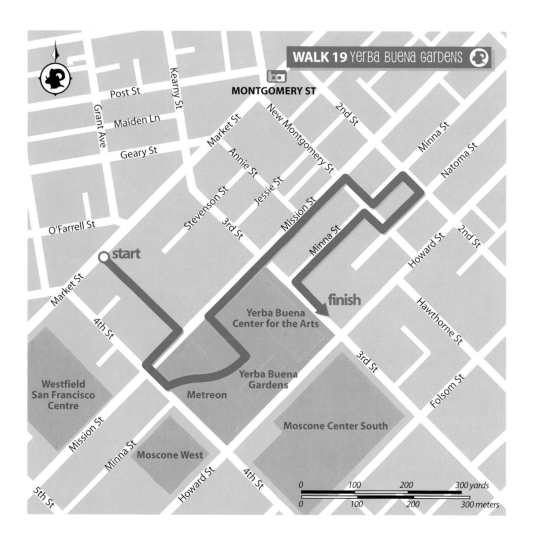

WALK 19 Yerba Buena Gardens

MONTGOMERY ST

Post St

Kearny St

Grant Ave

Maiden Ln

Geary St

Market St

New Montgomery St

2nd St

Minna St

Natoma St

Annie St

Stevenson St

Jessie St

Mission St

Minna St

Howard St

2nd St

O'Farrell St

start

Yerba Buena
Center for the Arts

finish

Market St

4th St

3rd St

Hawthorne St

3rd St

Folsom St

Westfield
San Francisco
Centre

Metreon

Yerba Buena
Gardens

Mission St

Moscone Center South

Minna St

Moscone West

Howard St

4th St

5th St

| 0 | 100 | 200 | 300 yards |
| 0 | 100 | 200 | 300 meters |

19 Yerba Buena Gardens: Art Walk

BOUNDARIES: **Market St., 4th St., 2nd St., Natoma St.**
DISTANCE: **1 mile**
DIFFICULTY: **Easy**
PARKING: **5th and Mission garage**
PUBLIC TRANSIT: **15, 30, and 45 Muni buses; Market St. buses and streetcars;**
Powell St. BART station

This is a walking tour that involves very little walking. There's lots to see in this densely packed part of the South of Market area, which since the 1990s has become concentrated with museums. So rather than hitting the pavement and breezing past the sites on this tour, we'll actually enter some of them to enjoy interesting art. (We'll skip most, to avoid art fatigue.) Along the way, we'll check out notable buildings, a shopping mall, and a public plaza.

- Begin in front of the Four Seasons Hotel on Market St., between 3rd and 4th streets. The narrow pedestrian path to the right of the hotel is called Yerba Buena Lane and cuts directly to Mission St. and Yerba Buena Gardens. Halfway down it, the Museum of Craft and Folk Art is a sleek, modern space for interesting exhibits of outsider art as well as traditional crafts such as pottery. It's the exhibits that are worth going in for. As an example, a past exhibit highlighted works by Japanese immigrants interred in camps during World War II, which reflected the role of art in coping with that injustice. Admission is $5.

- At the end of Yerba Buena Lane turn right on Mission St. Here you're almost directly beneath the gleaming tower of the San Francisco Marriott Hotel, a much reviled piece of architecture that invariably is referred to as the "jukebox." There is a vague resemblance, but in truth, the building would probably be more likeable if it looked more like a jukebox and less like a hotel.

● Cross to the other side of Mission St., where the cool Metreon shopping center opened in 1999, at the height of the Dot-com frenzy. Hence the late '90s vibe. The shops mostly cater to the tastes of the multimedia age, and they include a large multiplex cinema, a PlayStation store where you can test drive new games, a Sony Style store filled with electronic gizmos, and a "Hall of Game" that honors the achievements of video game heroes. There's also a bookstore that sells the smartly designed books published by Chronicle Books—it's a shop without walls that seems designed to ensnare unwary shoppers who drift into it. (Apparently it's following the strategy of airport duty free shops.) While in the mall, say hello to Robby the Robot, the "famous and adored" (quoting sign here) movie robot whose credits include a starring role in the film *Forbidden Planet* and an appearance in the TV show *Lost in Space.* You'll find Robby on the ground floor, next to the elevators.

● Walk through the Metreon and exit through doors on the east side, facing Yerba Buena Gardens. The park is essentially an undulating lawn and a few trees, but it's a lovely urban space enhanced by an attractive skyline. Wander over to the elegant Martin Luther King Jr. Memorial, where a series of waterfalls pounds rocks below and drowns out your thoughts. Walk behind the falls to fully experience this reflective monument.

● The Yerba Buena Center for the Arts, on the 3rd St. side of the park, houses exhibit spaces and a performing arts center. Although YBCA's galleries are spacious and well lit, this is not your ivory tower sort of museum. It emphasizes the work of living artists in all manner of media, mostly with a local angle. Admission is $6.

● Exit the Garden on the Mission St. side. Across the street you'll see St. Patrick's Church, which was built in 1872. It was originally the Parish of Irish Catholics who lived in the immediate vicinity. Cross the street and enter the church for a look at the stained-glass windows and a humble exhibit of historic photos. Some members of the predominantly Filipino congregation here may be lighting votive candles or crawling, in a display of humility, up the aisles toward the altar.

● A few doors down, you'll either see construction of the new Jewish Museum in progress or, if it's already 2008, it will be fully built and you can walk over to check it out. High-profile architect Daniel Liebeskind designed the building, finding time to do so while winning the contract for the new World Trade Center towers in New York. He incorporated a historic power station in the design, which is otherwise marked by his trademark jagged style. The museum itself has galleries devoted to art, history, and ideas, all relating to the Jewish people.

● Next door to the Jewish Museum, plans are afoot for a huge new Mexican Museum. The project has remained in limbo for some years, but perhaps by the time of your walk construction will be underway.

● On the next block, between 3rd and New Montgomery streets, are three museums. First is the Museum of the African Diaspora, which exhibits the work of African and African-descended artists (admission $10). Back across the street is the California Historical Society, a stodgy and professorial establishment that serves primarily as a research facility with a huge library and a collection of historic photos. It plucks gems from its collections for display in the shop, and also offers some select souvenirs and books for sale. Admission is $3.

● The highlight of this block of Mission St. is the Cartoon Art Museum. The collection includes original drawings and inkings by a wide range of cartoon and comic artists. Old Little Nemo and Alley Oop strips share wall space with works by Chuck Jones, Charles M. Schulz, R. Crumb, and even a few Manga artists. You'll spot cels from Disney films as well as the adult-oriented underground comix. It's a unique museum that really belongs here in San Francisco. Schulz (creator of Charlie Brown) hailed from north of the city and helped get the museum started. Crumb and *Ghost World* creator Daniel Clowes and a host of others have lived in and around the city. Admission is $6.

Yerba Buena sculpture by John Roloff

- At New Montgomery turn right, and then make a left on narrow Minna St. On the corner of Minna and 2nd, 111 Minna St. Gallery is an elegant space that usually has interesting art exhibits going on. The gallery is also a nightclub, with DJ's spinning cool grooves for a savvy, arty crowd in the evening.

- Turn right on 2nd and then right on Natoma St., another narrow, in-between street. (SoMa's grid is marked by broad thoroughfares, widely spaced, with these narrow streets cutting through mid-block.) Turn right on New Montgomery, where the striking art deco high-rise on the other side, at No. 140, is the Pacific Telephone & Telegraph Building. It was designed by Timothy Pfleuger and James Miller and built in 1925. Enter the lobby and gaze up at the intriguing Orientalist motif etched into the ceiling.

- Turn left on Minna and follow it back to 3rd St. and the San Francisco Museum of Modern Art, or SFMoMA as it's commonly called. Designed by Mario Botta, the museum moved to these new digs in 1995 after residing in the Civic Center for many decades. It's an exceedingly popular museum, although many local art enthusiasts grumble that its permanent collection could be so much better. Its photography collection is excellent, and fine traveling exhibits regularly stop here. The space is sleek and fun, and the cafeteria, Caffe Museo, is a happening spot for lunching and people watching. Admission to the museum is $12.50.

POINTS OF INTEREST

Museum of Craft and Folk Art 51 Yerba Buena Lane, 415-227-4888

Yerba Buena Center for the Arts 701 Mission St., 415-978-2787 (closed Monday)

Museum of the African Diaspora 685 Mission St., 415-358-7200 (closed Tuesday)

California Historical Society 678 Mission St., 415-357-1848 (closed Sunday–Tuesday)

Cartoon Art Museum 655 Mission St., 415-227-8666 (closed Monday)

111 Minna St. Gallery 111 Minna St., 415-974-1719

SFMoMA 151 3rd St., 415-357-4000

route summary

1. Begin by walking southeast off Market St., down Yerba Buena Lane, a pedestrian link from Market St. to Mission St.
2. At Mission St., turn right, to the corner of 4th and Mission streets.
3. Cross Mission St. and enter the Metreon.
4. Exit the Metreon on the east side, which leads directly into Yerba Buena Gardens.
5. Exit the gardens on the Mission St. side.
6. Cross Mission St. and turn right.
7. Turn right on New Montgomery St.
8. Turn left on Minna St.
9. Turn right on 2nd St.
10. Turn right on Natoma St.
11. Turn right on New Montgomery St.
12. Turn left on Minna St.
13. Turn right on 3rd St.

Duboce Park

start

Castro St

14th St

Henry St

15th St

Beaver St

States St

Flint St

Walter St

Sanchez St

Belcher St

Church St

Market St

Landers St

Church St

Market St

Pond St

Ford St

17th St

Dorland St

18th St

Hancock St

19th St

Cumberland St

Liberty St

Hill St

22nd St

Alvarado St

23rd St

Douglass St

Diamond St

21st St

20th St

Hartford St

Castro St

Collingwood St

Diamond St

19th St

Eureka St

Noe St

Sanchez St

Vicksburg St

Church St

finish

Quane St

Dolores St

Fair Oaks St

Guerrero St

San Jose Ave

24th St

Jersey St

Mission Dolores Park

Dolores St

Guerrero St

14th St

15th St

16th St

17th St

Julian Ave

Linda St

Valencia St

Lexington St

San Carlos St

18th St

19th St

20th St

21st St

Hill St

Bartlett St

22nd St

Capp St

Van Ness Ave

Mission St

Van Ness Ave

Shotwell St

16th St

16TH ST MISSION

24TH ST MISSION

0   200   400   600 yards

0   200   400   600 meters

20 DOLORES STREET: HIGH-TONED SIDE OF THE MISSION

BOUNDARIES: **Market St., Valencia St., 24th St., Sanchez St.**
DISTANCE: **2½ miles**
DIFFICULTY: **Strenuous (uphill climbs)**
PARKING: **Street parking is limited to two hours except on Sunday. The Market and Noe Garage (261 Noe St.) is three blocks from the start of this tour. Do not park at the Safeway across the street, as it is monitored.**
PUBLIC TRANSIT: **F streetcar; J Church train**

Dolores St. is luxuriant without being snooty, grand but not opulent. For some 2 miles, the street's palm-shaded median follows a straight and gracefully undulating path along the eastern edge of the Mission District. A walk along it takes in the Mission Dolores, the panoramic vistas from Dolores Park, and inviting tangents up and down some of San Francisco's finest rows of 19th century houses. It skirts the fringes of the Castro and Noe Valley. Apart from the Mission itself, this tour is not hugely concerned with landmarks or history. It's just one of the most beautiful walks in the city. We won't faithfully walk every block of Dolores St., opting instead to venture into the rollercoaster blocks of the Liberty Hill District and the northern rim of Noe Valley.

● Start at the corner of Dolores and Market streets, where the *California Volunteers* statue appears poised to ward off an invading army. The statue is worth a moment's appreciation, for it was created by Douglas Tilden, one of the city's finest artists at the turn of the 20th century. Tilden is widely known locally for works with somewhat overt homoerotic appeal, but this one, so near the Castro, is far more restrained. It's very dramatic, though, with its cavalryman jabbing the air with his sword as his wild-eyed horse tramples a fallen soldier.

● Walk down Dolores St. Once you're past the huge car dealership, the street begins to take on its elegant character. Most of the buildings on either side of the street are apartment buildings. The palms in the medians are popular pit stops for wild parrots. (The flocks here do not mingle with the flocks that habituate Telegraph Hill and parks in the north half of the city.)

- At 16th St., the huge Mission Dolores Basilica rises into view, and behind it is the humble Mission itself. The Mission Dolores, built of four-foot-thick adobe walls and a clay tile roof supported by wood beams, is the oldest building in San Francisco, having been completed by 1791. When the mission was founded in 1776 it originally stood about a block and a half east of here, on the shore of Laguna de los Dolores, an inland waterway that was filled in long ago. The Spanish missionaries conscripted local Indians to do their building for them, more or less in exchange for saving their souls. The surrounding lands were farmed by Indians along with Spanish families, though the settlement remained very small. The much larger Basilica was built after the 1906 fires destroyed an earlier cathedral on the site. Pope John Paul II said mass here on September 17, 1987. By all means, pay the $5 admission and take a self-guided tour. Beside the mission, the cemetery is a highlight, in part because it is the only non-military cemetery within the city limits. Most of the names are worn off the ancient headstones, but interred here is an intriguing mix of dignitaries, paupers, and ordinary Joe's from the 18th and 19th centuries.

- At the corner of 18th and Dolores, the Dolores Park Cafe is a congenial spot for a light and healthy lunch or refreshment. The sidewalk tables are highly sought-after on weekends, but you might easily snag one on a weekday. Or save this spot for a Friday night, when live musicians perform inside.

- Two blocks down Dolores St., Mission High School's bell towers are a nice complement to the mission. Built in the Mission Revival style, construction of the school was completed in 1924. Author Maya Angelou and rocker Carlos Santana are alums.

- For the next few blocks, Dolores Park slopes up from the western side of the street. It's an amphitheater-like bank of green, with tennis courts, a soccer pitch, a playground, and lawns that are very popular among dog walkers and sunbathers. Continue on the sidewalk for a block, then follow the asphalt walkway up through the park toward the statue of Miguel Hidalgo, liberator of Mexico in 1810 (which, of course, included California at the time). Beyond the Hidalgo statue, cross the pedestrian bridge, which clears the Muni J Church streetcar tracks, then make a left onto the sidewalk just below Church St. The corner of Church and 20th is the southwest corner of the park and one of the great lookout points in SF. The J Church train is a pleasure to ride (you might want to catch one at the end of this walk) for views like this, as well as for the curving course the tracks follow through the backyards of the neighborhood.

- Turn left on 20th St., following the southern edge of the park, then turn right on Dolores. A block down, turn left on Liberty St. The south side of the block is a fine row of historic houses, all very different in style and all in tip-top shape. At Guerrero St., turn right. On the corner of 21st St., the house at 900 Guerrero is a stunner built by John Daly, a dairy farmer, in 1895. Parts of Daly City, named for him, were developed on land that had been his farm. The house here is in excellent condition, although it is no longer a single-family home.

- Turn left on Hill St. On the north side of the block is an impeccable row of nearly identical stick-style Victorians, all built in the 1870s and '80s. These were originally middle-class homes.

- Turn left on Valencia St. and left again on 21st St., which we'll follow past Dolores St. up to Church St. At Church turn right, then turn left on Liberty. It's a steady climb to the top. Stay on the north side of the street, where you can see the gardens that appear to be thriving along the median—hopefully, the sight of plants will make the uphill trudge easier to bear. At the top of the block, take the steps leading to Sanchez St. and turn left.

- A block up, the corner house at 3690 21st St. is a gingerbread cottage straight out of a classic Disney feature. It's called Casa Ciele ("sky house" in Spanish), which ought to feel appropriate enough if you're suffering from altitude sickness after hiking up to this point.

Mission Dolores

● It's all downhill from here, in a purely topographical sense. Follow Sanchez several blocks to 24th St., where you turn left to reach the shopping strip of Noe Valley. The neighborhood is an enclave of millionaire couples, each raising one kid, and the street mostly serves local needs. You might have a good cup of coffee or spoil yourself by purchasing a new pair of designer shoes. For the best dining, backtrack to the corner of Douglass St., where Firefly serves up deservedly celebrated New American cuisine. To get back to where you started, turn left at Church St. and hop on a J train for a scenic ride.

POINTS OF INTEREST

Mission Dolores 3321 16th St., 415-621-8203

Dolores Park Cafe 501 Dolores St., 415-621-2936

Firefly Restaurant 4288 24th St., 415-821-7652

route summary

1. Start at the Market St. end of Dolores St. and head south, to 16th St. and the Mission Dolores.
2. Continue south, to Dolores Park
3. Midway through Dolores Park, turn right up the asphalt path which leads to Church St.
4. Turn left at Church St.
5. Turn left at 20th St.
6. Turn right at Dolores St.
7. Turn left at Liberty St.
8. Turn right at Guerrero St.
9. Turn left at Hill St.
10. Turn left at Valencia St.
11. Turn left at 21st St.
12. Turn right at Church St.
13. Turn left at Liberty St.
14. Turn left at Sanchez St.

Victorian beauty, Liberty Hill District

21 THE INNER MISSION: TACOS AND TATTOO'D BUILDINGS

BOUNDARIES: **16th St., Dolores St., 25th St., York St.**
DISTANCE: **2¼ miles**
DIFFICULTY: **Easy**
PARKING: **Off-street parking is available on the corner of Valencia and 18th streets.**
PUBLIC TRANSIT: **16th St. and 24th St. BART stations; 14 Muni bus.**

San Francisco's most vibrant, diverse, and creative neighborhood is the Mission. The broad, flat district is populated by Latino families, artsy hipsters, and a growing number of white-collar workers. Amid the bars, bodegas, taquerías, and upscale restaurants are many buildings distinguished not so much by the businesses operating there, but by the art on the exterior walls. Murals—some in the tradition of Diego Rivera, others drawing on contemporary pop culture—have proliferated throughout the Mission. There are far too many works of art to take in on a single walk. This walk passes many of the key murals, and ducks into a few shops to get a feel for the neighborhood.

● Start at the corner of Mission and 16th streets, which is convenient if you're arriving on a BART train. Unfortunately, this busy intersection seems to be getting more depressing with each year, as the immediate area becomes the end of the line for a growing number of junkies and prostitutes. Walk a block east on 16th and you'll reach the Redstone Building, at No. 2926. This building, also called the "Temple of Labor," is a meeting hall for labor unions. During business hours, enter to view the murals that cover every inch of wall space in the lobby and hallways. The murals, including works by Barry McGee, Rigo, Aaron Noble, John Fadeff, and Sebastiana Pastor, were unveiled in 1997. Many of the works here echo the styles of the Depression-era artists who contributed pro-labor murals in Coit Tower and elsewhere in the city. The artists who worked on the Redstone Building are all associated with the Clarion Alley Mural Project (CAMP), and we'll see more of their works on the next stop of this tour.

- Return to Mission St. and, after crossing, turn left on Mission and right onto narrow Clarion Alley. This open-air gallery, which covers nearly every building between Mission and Valencia Sts., is an ongoing project that was started in the early 1990s by the Clarion Alley Mural Project. Two of CAMP's original members, Aaron Noble and Rigo, lived in an artists' warehouse near the Valencia St. end of the alley until the building was demolished in 2001. Along with the building, some terrific art was lost, but the new townhouse on the site is already covered with murals. The works here are of varying styles, ranging from traditional Mexican techniques to more contemporary comic-book and graffiti styles.

- At Valencia turn right and then turn left at 17th St. Make a left at Dearborn St. As you approach 18th St., the spectacular Women's Building comes into view. An enormous mural, called *Maestrapeace,* wraps like vines around two sides of the building. It was painted in 1994 by seven women artists, and thematically the painting celebrates women of all cultures. Walk a little ways up Lapidge St. to see the artwork on the building's east side.

- Return to 18th St. and turn right. The building on the corner of 18th and

Backstory: Kinky Stuff

In December 2006, a historic building in the Mission District was sold. The building is the old State Armory and Arsenal, a huge pile at 1800 Mission St. that was designed to resemble a Moorish Castle. The buyer is Kink, producer of bondage films. So, just when people were starting to worry that the Mission was getting less interesting, along comes the porn industry to the rescue.

Kink announced it would use the site as a production studio for its fetish films. The building seems strikingly well suited to the purpose. It looks menacing from the street, and it has a dungeon-like basement and stone stairwells. According to filmmaker James Mogul, the boiler room has been waiting decades for a chance to serve as a set.

Lexington streets (on the Lex side) is covered with one of the neighborhood's more intriguing works. It's called *Generator*, and the artists are Andrew Schoultz and Aaron Noble. It's a finely crafted and unusual work, with cross-hatch shading and images of strange, intertwined birdhouses lurching skyward. It looks like something Dr. Seuss might have conjured up in one of his more harrowing tales. Note the way the artists incorporated the building's ventilation pipes and the power lines that cross in front of the painting. It's fun, intricate, and thought-provoking.

● Follow Lexington to 19th St. and turn left. Turn right onto Mission St., one of San Francisco's liveliest and most interesting streets. Amid the taquerías and tiendas you'll see signs of the street's pre-Latino past, when this was a largely Irish neighborhood. Some blocks are dominated by the faded and rusted beacons of grand old movie palaces that closed down decades ago. To get a real feel for the street, have a veggie burrito at Taquería Can-Cun (between 18th and 19th streets) or a carnitas taco at La Taquería (between 24th and 25th streets). Also, duck into Mission Market, a smorgasbord of spices, salsas, and produce for the Mexican American kitchen. The market opens up into a small indoor mall, where tables are set in the middle and food stalls sell plate lunches and raspados. On a busy day, it has the spirit and atmosphere of a market in Mexico.

● Turn left onto shady 24th St., lined with shops, restaurants, and cantinas, almost all catering to the Latin American community. A few blocks down, turn right onto Balmy Alley, the Mecca of the Mission District's mural arts scene. It's your classic back alley lined with garage doors and backyard fences, but just about the entire length of it is covered with colorful murals in a great variety of styles. The oldest works are from the

Balmy Alley mural

1970s and tend to address social issues in Latin America and in the local community. The influence of Diego Rivera and Jose Clemente Orozco is strongly evident. Georgia O'Keefe appears to have inspired some of the artists as well. Some of the more contemporary works are by artists cut from the Clarion Alley cloth, and while not necessarily apolitical, are stylistically less tied to the traditions of the Latin American left. Some works make use of stencils, while others are inspired by cinema and comics. New murals appear all the time. Walk to the end of the block and back, taking in the art along both sides of the alley, and continue down 24th St.

- Half a block down, at No. 2981, is the Precita Eyes Art Store and Visitors Center, which is a great place for learning about the local mural arts scene. Founded in 1977 by muralist Susan Cervantes, Precita Eyes has overseen many important commissions throughout the neighborhood, including along Balmy Alley, and the center's educational wing has produced many of the Mission's artists. The shop sells postcard photos of murals and T-shirts with murals on them. Anyone wishing to delve deeper into the culture can gather books and information here.

- Across the street, past Alabama St., are a couple of very traditional Latino markets. Casa Lucas, at No. 2934, is a colorful shop that's useful if you're in need of a piñata or a bottle of guava juice. On the corner of Florida St., at No. 2884, La Palma Mexicatessen is a no-nonsense purveyor of over-the-counter snacks, including excellent tamales and tacos. Grab a pack of hand-patted corn tortillas for an authentic treat. Sometimes, you can spot women making them in the back of the shop.

- At the corner of 24th and Bryant streets, Galería de la Raza is a neighborhood institution that was founded in 1970 by artists involved in the Chicano civil rights movement. The gallery is an interdisciplinary space where art is exhibited and performances are staged. The gallery often showcases provocative and controversial art that usually casts perspective on topical issues such as illegal immigration.

- A block down 24th St., we can end our tour over a milkshake at St. Francis Fountain, a classic ice cream shop that hasn't bothered to maintain Smithsonian-quality decor but is more comfortable for it. You can also get a burger or B.L.T. if you haven't already filled up on Mexican food.

POINTS OF INTEREST

Redstone Building 2926 16th St.

Women's Building 3543 18th St., 415-431-1180

Mission Market Fish & Poultry 2590 Mission St., 415-282-3331

Taquería Can-Cun 2288 Mission St., 415-252-9560

La Taquería 2889 Mission St., 415-285-7117

Precita Eyes Art Store & Visitors Center 2981 24th St., 415-285-2287

Casa Lucas Market 2934 24th St., 415-593-0785

La Palma Mexica-tessen 2884 24th St., 415-647-1500

Galería de la Raza 2857 24th St., 415-826-8009

St. Francis Fountain 2801 24th St., 415-826-4200

ROUTE SUMMARY

1. Start at the corner of Mission and 16th streets.
2. Head east on 16th St., cross Capp St., and enter the Redstone Building.
3. Return via 16th St. to Mission St., cross Mission St., and turn left.
4. Turn left off Mission onto Clarion Alley.
5. Turn right on Valencia St.
6. Turn left on 17th St.
7. Turn left on Dearborn St.
8. Turn left on 18th St.
9. Turn right on Lexington St.
10. Turn left on 19th St.
11. Turn right on Mission St.
12. Turn left on 24th St.
13. Turn right on Balmy Alley, walk a block up and back, returning to 24th St.
14. Continue on 24th St. and stop at York St.

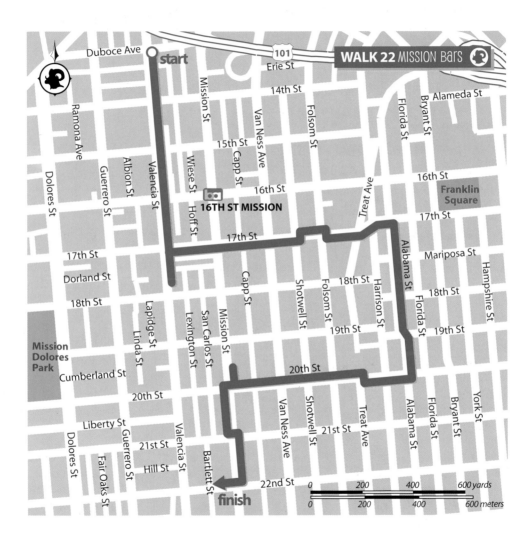

22 MISSION BARS: HAPPY HOURS, HAPPY FEET

BOUNDARIES: **Duboce St., Valencia St., Folsom St., 22nd St.**
DISTANCE: **2¼ miles**
DIFFICULTY: **Easy**
PARKING: **Street parking, which can be difficult to find, is unlimited in the evening. There is off-street parking at the corner of 18th and Valencia streets.**
PUBLIC TRANSIT: **F streetcar; 16th St. BART station; 26 Muni bus**

As the sun goes down on the Mission District the neighborhood's vibrant murals fade into the shadows and irresistible artificial light splashes out onto sidewalks from the barrooms. This is one of the city's very best nightlife zones. The entertainment options are varied and of high quality, with a healthy mix of dives, supper clubs, and live-music venues. This tour selects several scattered spots, and you'll no doubt want to whittle the list down a little further to avoid ending up in a gutter somewheres. A lot of ground is covered, and some of the streets are a bit dodgy at night. Use good sense while walking down dark blocks. You might also want to break a cardinal rule of walking tours and call on a taxi to bridge the gaps now and then.

- A fine place to start is Zeitgeist, where bikers and tattoo'd punk rockers hang out, on the corner of Valencia St. and Duboce Ave. The draw here, really, is the outdoor beer garden, which is nothing more than a graveled lot with picnic tables and a freeway ramp looming above it. Somehow, in the twilight on a warmish evening, this is one of the best places to be in San Francisco. The unassuming environs have a neutralizing effect on people who might not always share the same attitudes—meaning you needn't be a local, a biker, or tattoo'd to feel at home here. You can grab a greasy burger and similar fare from a window next to the pool table.

- Before you get too comfortable out in Zeitgeist's backyard, head down Valencia St. several blocks, to the Elbo Room, on Valencia between 17th and 18th streets. The bar has been operating in some capacity or other since the end of Prohibition, but it has been a Mission District hipster magnet since the early '90s. If you can snare a stool at the sexy, curvaceous bar then you deserve a suave cocktail of some kind. When things get cranking here—9 or 10 p.m., usually—it can be difficult to get anywhere near a bartender or a server. Bands (rock, Latin, misc.) and DJs work the room upstairs. Have an early drink, return to 17th St., turn right, and mosey on.

- Next stop is the Uptown, at 17th and Capp streets. No part of San Francisco is known as Uptown, but why quibble over a name. This is one of the city's great dives. It doesn't look particularly welcoming from the outside (extra points for that) and the location couldn't be worse (more extra points), but step in and you'll have a hard time leaving (jackpot points). The old Formica booths and cool lighting could have been assembled by a savvy film-set designer, but this place feels too real for that. It's very low key and more of a local than most of the hip Mission joints. Play some pinball or shoot some pool before moving on.

- A little farther down, on the desolate corner of 17th and Folsom streets, is the unas- suming Rite Spot. From the outside the bar appears to have been closed for years. It's a great look. Inside is about the same, slightly sleepy, slightly uncared for. Also slightly surreal. It's a supper club, with a long bar and a mess of tables and barely enough space for the band. The bands are of all stripes, and whoever books 'em is clearly bored with contemporary mainstream music. You can order Italian-American dishes— have the chicken cacciatore sandwich lathered in melted cheese and mayonnaise.

- From the Rite Spot follow 17th St. to Alabama St., turn right and continue to 20th St. The Atlas Cafe has been holding down this corner since 1996. If it's past 10 p.m., though, skip this part of the tour. If it's a Thursday night, definitely make this stop, since that's when the Atlas features live bluegrass music. It's a low-key, slightly arty coffee shop with an upbeat vibe. You can order beer, pizzas, and good sandwiches.

- Turning right onto 20th St., return to Mission St. The next couple of blocks have enough bars for a weeklong bender. Just north of Mission, off 20th you can't miss Bruno's bold, lit-up sign. It opened in the 1940s as a clubby Italian-American res- taurant with sleek lines, mood lighting, and plush Naugahyde booths. In the '90s the place benefited from renewed interest in mid-20th century swank and highball culture. An intimate jazz room was added. Recently Bruno's pared down its menu (burgers, mainly) and introduced club nights on the weekend; weeknights are rela- tively quiet.

- Turning around and heading south to the next block of Mission, between 20th and 21st streets, you come to Medjool, a relative newcomer, having opened in the 21st century. It's trendy and crowded, which can make it interesting and unpleasant at the same time. If the weather is nice, head up to the rooftop patio, where full bar service is available. In the downstairs lounge, you can order from a Mediterranean menu that covers the entire region's cuisine, from Southern Europe on around to North Africa.

- If you're still in a fashionable-contemporary mood, next door is Foreign Cinema, a one-stop shop for dinner and a movie. Just slip into the sultry Laszlo Bar for sophisticated concoctions and cool DJs after 9 p.m.

- Down the road a piece is 12 Galaxies, one of the city's best small live music venues. The place has a solid reputation for booking indie artists who are on the cusp of gaining a national audience. There's usually a cover for the shows, but if you get here early enough you can enter free and drink at the bar until the music starts (usually 9 p.m.). It's a nice, open space, contemporary in feel without hitting you over the head with style.

- A few doors down from 12 Galaxies is another of the Mission's fine dives, Doc's Clock. Before entering, walk across the street to admire the sign, a real beauty that promises good times within. On past the seductively lit bar is a little room where you can drink and play shuffleboard. On rare occasions (usually Tuesday night) there's live music performed by old crackpots with an eclectic repertoire. No cover.

- Turn right at 22nd St. The Make-Out Room, just off the corner, is a fine and idiosyncratic watering hole that's been a neighborhood stalwart for over

Doc's Clock

a decade now. With an assemblage of Formica tables scattered over a concrete floor, it's nothing fancy, but the joint still has atmosphere and a certain amount of class. Many nights after 8 p.m. it features live bands—everything from cowpunk to indie rock—and charges a cover.

● If the music scene at the Make-Out doesn't steam your glasses, head up the block to the Latin American Club, an equally unfussy yet appealing bar. These are distinctive and tranquil environs with a Mission-slacker bent—it's a good spot to settle into over conversation.

POINTS OF INTEREST

Zeitgeist 199 Valencia St., 415-255-7505

Elbo Room 647 Valencia St., 415-552-7788

Uptown 200 Capp St., 415-861-8231

Rite Spot 2099 Folsom St., 415-552-6066

Atlas Cafe 3049 20th St., 415-648-1047

Bruno's 2389 Mission St., 415-643-5200

Medjool 2522 Mission St., 415-550-9055

Foreign Cinema 534 Mission St., 415-648-7600

12 Galaxies 2565 Mission St., 415-970-9777

Doc's Clock 2575 Mission St., 415-824-3627

Make-Out Room 3225 22nd St., 415-2888

Latin American Club 3286 22nd St., 415-647-2732

route summary

1. Start at the Zeitgeist, corner of Valencia St. and Duboce Ave.

2. Head south on Valencia St., past 17th St., and you'll reach the Elbo Room.

3. Return to 17th St. and turn right. A block past Mission St., at Capp St., is the Uptown.

4. Continue on 17th St. At the corner of Folsom St., is the Rite Spot.

5. Continue on 17th St. to Alabama St. and turn right.

6. At 20th St. turn left. Just off the corner is the Atlas Cafe.

7. Turn around and follow 20th St. west.

8. Turn right at Mission St. Just off the corner is Bruno's.

9. Turn around and head south on Mission St. Just past 20th St. are Medjool and Laszlo.

10. Continue on Mission St. On the other side of the street, past 21st St., is 12 Galaxies and Doc's Clock.

11. Turn right on 22nd St. Just off the corner is the Make-Out Room.

12. Continue on 22nd St. Near the corner of Valencia is the Latin American Club.

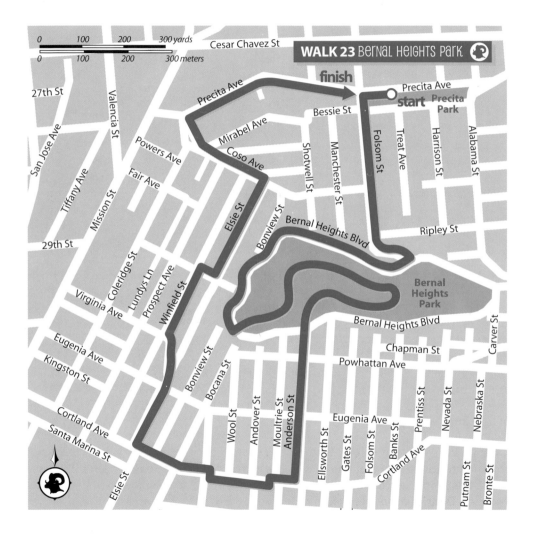

WALK 23 Bernal Heights Park

finish

start

Precita Park

Bernal Heights Park

0 100 200 300 yards
0 100 200 300 meters

Cesar Chavez St

Precita Ave
Bessie St
Precita Ave

27th St

Valencia St

San Jose Ave

Mission St

Tiffany Ave

Powers Ave

Fair Ave

Mirabel Ave

Coso Ave

Shotwell St

Manchester St

Folsom St

Treat Ave

Harrison St

Alabama St

Elsie St

Bonview St

Bernal Heights Blvd

Ripley St

29th St

Coleridge St

Lundys Ln

Prospect Ave

Winfield St

Virginia Ave

Bonview St

Bocana St

Bernal Heights Blvd

Chapman St

Carver St

Eugenia Ave

Kingston St

Powhattan Ave

Wool St

Andover St

Moultrie St

Anderson St

Ellsworth St

Eugenia Ave

Gates St

Folsom St

Banks St

Cortland Ave

Prentiss St

Nevada St

Nebraska St

Cortland Ave

Santa Marina St

Elsie St

Putnam St

Bronte St

23 Bernal Heights Park: a Dog's Fondest Dream

BOUNDARIES: **Precita Ave., Folsom St., Cortland Ave., Winfield St.**
DISTANCE: **2 miles**
DIFFICULTY: **Moderate (long uphill stretches)**
PARKING: **Street parking around Precita Park has no time restriction.**
PUBLIC TRANSIT: **12, 14, and 27 Muni buses; 24th St. BART station**

Bernal Heights rises up from the southern edge of the Mission, where narrow streets dead-end long before they can reach this rocky, windswept hilltop. The broad views of the Mission, Potrero Hill, the bay, and the distant downtown skyline are fantastic—but that's par for the course in San Francisco. What makes this walk especially alluring is the suddenness with which the sheltered, slightly funky Bernal Heights neighborhood turns into a rugged chunk of wilderness. The hill is home to many red-tailed hawks, which glide silently about the slopes looking for anything small that moves. Wear good hiking shoes for this one. And if you have a dog handy, bring it along and free it from its leash—you'll both fit right in.

● Start at Precita Park, in a pleasant residential pocket to the north of Bernal. You can grab a cup of coffee at one of the cafes on tree-lined Folsom St., which runs along the park's western edge. Turn left, heading south. Folsom rises steadfastly, as though developers entertained thoughts of making it clear the hill in a straight shot. However, within two blocks, as the going gets rough, the road abruptly swerves to the left. Just as suddenly, you're above the rooftops, amid the grassy, rocky terrain for which Bernal Heights is known. If it's the rainy season, wind, clouds, and mist swirl about the green face of the hill. In spring, the hill is covered with wildflowers. In summer, its an arid scape of red rock and yellow grasses. There's a dog for just about every human up here.

● Folsom curves up to Bernal Heights Blvd. Turn right, pass the gate (which prohibits cars from going further), and you'll enter Bernal Heights Park. The road loops up a fairly easy incline around the hill. The long, straight boulevards that slice through the Mission District drop into view behind you. Down below the road, along the western side of the hill, look out for narrow, unofficial trails (which at times fade beneath new grass or fallen pine needles)—these lead to hidden gardens planted by local residents on city property. The steps heading down to Esmerelda St. lead to some of these gardens.

- On the south side, where the road is gated, a wide, rocky path corkscrews up toward the top of the hill. The red rock here is chert, and is the same stuff found up on Corona Heights (see the Westside Cordillera walk). Follow the trail up. On blustery days, you might see several hawks hovering in place about 20 feet overhead, their wings stretched wide, adjusting perceptibly to keep the wind beneath them. The birds keep very still up there, stealthily scanning the ground for potential prey. Stand beneath them and you'll have about as good a look (without the aid of binoculars) as you could ever hope to get of wild raptors in action.

- The path loops around the summit, providing unbroken perspectives of the city and the bay. There are ledges and lookouts and little spur trails. It's not a huge area, but you'll want to roam about a bit before returning to Bernal Heights Blvd. A driveway leads down from the top. Look for Anderson St., and stroll on down past a hodgepodge of residential architectural styles. Bernal Heights was never a wealthy district, although today these homes sell for a pretty penny (as do all homes in SF). The narrow

BACK STORY: BERNAL CINEMA

Bernal Heights naturally attracts creative types, and to prove it, every fall the neighborhood showcases the works of local filmmakers in an outdoor film festival. Films are shown on Saturday nights during the months of September and October. The filmmakers usually give a talk in a local cafe, then everyone proceeds to a nearby park (sometimes Bernal Heights Park), where the film is shown as the sun goes down. It's a fun and social event.

The neighborhood's best known filmmaker is Terry Zweigoff, director of such delights as *Bad Santa* and *Ghost World*. So far, the festival hasn't featured any of Zweigoff's work. For information, check www.bhoutdoorcine.org.

streets, many of which curve abruptly to avoid steep grades, give the area an off-beat, Montmartre-like feel.

● Follow Anderson down to Cortland Ave., the main commercial strip. Make a right; you'll find good places to eat, coffee shops, and a bookstore. Bernal doesn't generally draw much business from out-of-towners or even from people who live elsewhere in the city, making this a very neighborly sort of urban backwater. That's not to say it's backwards, though. Fine restaurants here include Moki's Sushi and Pacific Grill (for sushi and Polynesian dishes), and the Liberty Cafe (where the chicken pot pie is legendary). Wild Side West is a funky Lesbian bar that often draws a mixed crowd simply because it's the best watering hole on the hill.

● As Cortland begins to descend back down to Mission St. turn right on Elsie St. Just off the corner, note the 19th-century barn that was converted into a house ages ago. Two blocks down, Virginia Ave. curves up to meet Elsie. Follow it and you'll see some of the neighborhood's finest Victorian homes. Local residents are cultivating a garden along the right side of the road, beneath the curved retaining wall. A block down, turn right on Winfield, which runs in a straight line to the north side of the hill. From here you can meander back to Precita Park, along the way discovering hidden pockets where the streets meet at odd angles. You have two straightforward choices: take a right on Coso Ave., which leads back to Folsom, or turn left on Coso and you'll soon reach pretty Mirabel Ave., which, if you turn right, gets you back to Precita Park.

View of the Mission District from Bernal Heights

POINTS OF INTEREST

Moki's Sushi and Pacific Grill 615 Cortland Ave., 415-970-9336

Liberty Cafe 10 Cortland Ave., 415-695-8777

Wild Side West 424 Cortland Ave., 415-647-3099

route summary

1. Begin at Precita Park and turn left up Folsom St.
2. Turn right onto Bernal Heights Blvd.; enter the park.
3. Pass the gate onto the dirt road, making your way around the summit of the hill.
4. Turn left (south) on Anderson St.
5. Turn right on Cortland Ave.
6. Turn right on Elsie St.
7. Turn left on Virginia St.
8. Turn right on Winfield St.
9. Take Coso Ave. right to Folsom St. or left to Mirabel Ave., either way returning to Precita Park.

Views from Bernal Heights

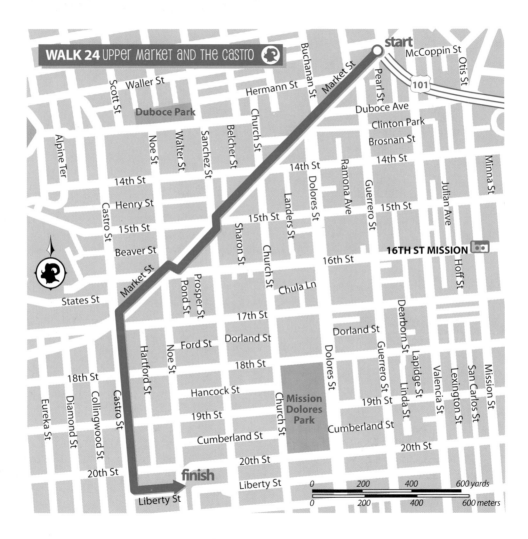

WALK 24 Upper market and the Castro

start

McCoppin St

Otis St

Buchanan St

Market St

Pearl St

101

Waller St

Hermann St

Duboce Ave

Scott St

Clinton Park

Duboce Park

Brosnan St

Minna St

14th St

Church St

Belcher St

Sanchez St

Walter St

Noe St

Alpine Ter

14th St

Dolores St

Ramona Ave

Guerrero St

15th St

Julian Ave

14th St

Henry St

Landers St

15th St

Castro St

Sharon St

15th St

Beaver St

Church St

16th St

16TH ST MISSION

Hoff St

Market St

Prosper St

Pond St

Chula Ln

States St

17th St

Ford St

Dorland St

Dorland St

Dearborn St

Lapidge St

Linda St

Dolores St

Guerrero St

Valencia St

Lexington St

San Carlos St

Mission St

Hartford St

Noe St

18th St

18th St

Hancock St

19th St

19th St

Mission Dolores Park

Church St

Cumberland St

Eureka St

Diamond St

Collingwood St

Castro St

19th St

Cumberland St

20th St

20th St

20th St

20th St

Liberty St

finish

Liberty St

Liberty St

| 0 | 200 | 400 | 600 yards |
| 0 | 200 | 400 | 600 meters |

24 Upper Market and the Castro: Gay Bars and Victorian Beauties

BOUNDARIES: Market St., Octavia St., Douglass St., 20th St.
DISTANCE: 1½ miles
DIFFICULTY: Easy
PARKING: You might try your luck along Guerrero or Valencia streets. Off-street parking is available at the Market and Noe Garage.
PUBLIC TRANSIT: F streetcar

The Castro is probably the best known gay neighborhood in the U.S. Perhaps not coincidentally, it's also a treasure trove of lovingly maintained architectural gems, with unbroken strings of beautiful Victorian houses along many blocks. Formally called Eureka Valley, the neighborhood was home to a middle-class immigrant community before gays began to drift out this way in the early 1970s. They were most likely drawn by the housing stock and the winning location, with streets terracing up the eastern slope of Twin Peaks, which on most days shields the Castro from the fog. The neighborhood's quiet residential streets reflect the refined tastes of its denizens, who are by and large established professionals. Castro St. between Market and 18th streets is the busy commercial hub, with Upper Market taking on much of the spillover. This tour will take in both sides of the district: the elegant homes as well as the bars and clubs that reflect the Castro's social side.

- Over the years, the gay community has spread a ways down Market St., toward Civic Center, so we'll begin our tour well east of Castro St., at the corner of Market and Octavia streets. Here, at 1800 Market, The Center stands like a portal to the neighborhood. It offers services and programs for lesbians, gays, bisexuals, and transgenders, and also has a cafe. The Center is architecturally interesting, as it consists of a historic Victorian, painted a solid and sober blue, that segues into a strikingly modern wing of tinted glass panels, which meet at oblique angles. It's a suitable introduction to the neighborhood, where an appreciation for the old does not reflect a fear of the new.

- Heading west on Market, a few blocks up, on the same side of the street, you come to the Mint Karaoke Lounge, a little neighborhood dive that gets its name from the nearby U.S. Mint, which can be seen soon after you pass the bar. The Mint is a popular nightclub that draws a fairly mixed crowd, though it appeals mostly to hams eager for their turn at the mic. The U.S. Mint, up on the hill, is a foreboding structure that looks more like a futuristic military installation than a place that once produced circulating currency. It was built in 1937, and today mostly churns out collectible coin sets.

- Just below the U.S. Mint is a Safeway supermarket that's more or less like any other Safeway except for its proximity to the Castro. People perusing the aisles in search of toothpaste or canned corn have noted that this place can be somewhat cruisy.

- Up Market a couple of blocks, just before the corner of Sanchez St., is Cafe du Nord. The name is French, the architecture is Alpine gingerbread, and the classy below-street-level joint is pure swank with a modern, hip edge. The onetime speakeasy is a mainstay on San Francisco's small-venue live music scene, with a regular lineup of independent acts, mostly local and mostly worth catching. Upstairs, the Swedish American Hall is no meatball parlor, but another excellent live music venue. It has the look and feel of a Masonic lodge, with heavy beams and lots of wood trim. Events are scheduled here infrequently, though.

- A block up, on the opposite side, Image Leather is your basic gay-oriented purveyor of leather goods. The store appears fairly unassuming, and even a little quaint, from the sidewalk, but in the "dungeon" the shop keeps a "museum" of sex toys. You'll have to ask for permission to venture down there.

- On the next block, Lime is an interesting combination of eatery and nightclub. The decor is straight off the set of *Sleeper*—a '70s vision of the future that's not particularly appetizing. But the joint jumps.

- Across Market St., at the corner of Noe St., Cafe Flore is a celebrated hangout where the patio tables are highly coveted on sunny days. As you can see, in construction it resembles a gardener's shed, though on a much larger scale. Potted greenery contributes to the effect. But Cafe Flore is really all about coffee, beer, light meals, seeing, and being seen. A block up is Catch, a well-regarded seafood restaurant.

- The corner of Market and Castro streets, where you turn left onto Castro, is naturally one of the principle crossroads of the neighborhood. A huge rainbow flag flaps in the wind from a pole high above Harvey Milk Plaza, at the southwest corner. Named for the assassinated city supervisor, the cramped little plaza is tucked between a building and the entry to the Muni station, but if your dogs are tired it offers a couple of benches.

- Across the street, Twin Peaks Tavern is known by younger guys as "the coffin" because people under the age of 50 seldom drink in it. The bar is famous for its untinted picture windows, which were a novelty for a gay bar in the early '70s. The bar was open long before then, having served a blue-collar clientele for several decades.

- The neighborhood's biggest landmark is the Castro Theater, a few doors up Castro St. from the Twin Peaks Tavern. There aren't many movie palaces of this sort left, which is why the Castro is treasured by all San Franciscans. The programming is eclectic, featuring a mix of independent films as well as fine prints of the classics. Often, the movie is preceded by an artful performance on the house organ, and on occasion the Castro will screen silent films with a live pit orchestra. Several film festivals take place here. The building, a Moorish flight of fancy, is particularly dramatic at night, when the marquee is lit up. It was built in 1922 and the plans were drawn by architect Timothy Pfueger.

- A couple of doors farther along, Cliff's Variety is the neighborhood hardware store. It's been open since the 1940s. As with the Safeway, a common sort of store is made extraordinary by virtue of its location. Along with the usual plumbing and electrical fixtures the store stocks

Victorians on Liberty St.

plaster moldings for restoring 100-year-old houses and all the kitchen and bath supplies a happy homemaker might be looking for. It also has a fine selection of goofy toys of the sort that appeal to nostalgic adults. On the same block, A Different Light Bookstore is the city's leading gay-oriented bookstore. Several nights a week authors read from their works here.

● The bookshop is just a few paces from the corner of Castro and 18th streets, which is considered the nexus of the neighborhood. There are restaurants and hangouts in either direction along 18th St., but continue on Castro. At No. 575, Harvey Milk operated his camera store during the 1970s. Milk and his partner lived upstairs, and Milk conducted his campaign for supervisor here. A bronze plaque on the sidewalk commemorates his contributions to the local community.

● Just past 19th St., Castro St. turns residential, with an impressive row of Victorian apartment buildings stacking up along the incline. Continue on Castro, then turn left on Liberty St., which looks much as it would have over a century ago. Immaculate single-family homes, nearly uniform in character, line both sides. These were middle-class homes originally but are worth a pretty penny now. If the architecture is a turn-on for you, just wander around the historic district and you'll get your fill.

POINTS OF INTEREST

The Center 1800 Market St., 415-865-5555

Safeway 2020 Market St., 415-861-7660

Mint Karaoke Lounge 1942 Market St., 415-626-4726

Cafe Du Nord 2170 Market St., 415-861-5016

Image Leather 2199 Market St., 415-621-7551

Lime 2247 Market St., 415-621-5256

Cafe Flore 2298 Market St., 415-621-8579

Twin Peaks Tavern 401 Castro St., 415-864-9470

Castro Theater 429 Castro St., 415-621-6120

Cliff's Variety Store 479 Castro St., 415-431-5365

A Different Light Bookstore 489 Castro St., 415-431-0891

route summary

1. Start at Market and Octavia streets and head west along Market St.
2. Turn left at Castro St.
3. Turn left at Liberty St.

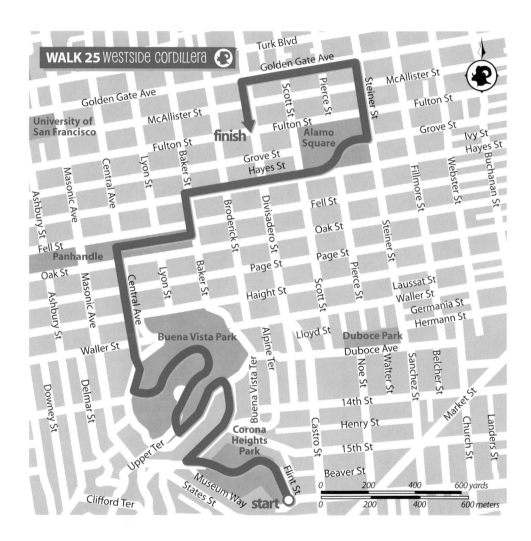

Turk Blvd

Golden Gate Ave

McAllister St

Fulton St

Grove St

Ivy St

Hayes St

Buchanan St

Webster St

Fillmore St

Steiner St

Pierce St

Scott St

Fulton St

finish

Alamo Square

Grove St

Hayes St

Golden Gate Ave

McAllister St

University of San Francisco

Fulton St

Lyon St

Baker St

Central Ave

Masonic Ave

Ashbury St

Fell St

Panhandle

Oak St

Ashbury St

Masonic Ave

Waller St

Downey St

Delmar St

Central Ave

Lyon St

Baker St

Broderick St

Divisadero St

Page St

Haight St

Fell St

Oak St

Page St

Scott St

Pierce St

Steiner St

Laussat St

Waller St

Germania St

Hermann St

Buena Vista Park

Alpine Ter

Lloyd St

Duboce Park

Duboce Ave

Noe St

Walter St

Sanchez St

Belcher St

Market St

Church St

Landers St

14th St

Henry St

15th St

Beaver St

Castro St

Buena Vista Ter

Corona Heights Park

Upper Ter

Flint St

Museum Way

States St

Clifford Ter

start

0   200   400   600 yards

0   200   400   600 meters

25 westside cordillera: corona HeiGHTS, BUeNa VISTa Park, aND alaMo SQUare

BOUNDARIES: **16th St., Central Ave., Golden Gate Ave., Steiner St.**
DISTANCE: **2½ miles**
DIFFICULTY: **Strenuous**
PARKING: **Two-hour street parking is available around Corona Heights, especially on 16th St. near the Flint St. entrance. Two hours doesn't leave enough time, so Sunday (when parking is unlimited) is a good day to make this walk. Off-street parking is available at the Market and Noe Garage, in the heart of the Castro.**
PUBLIC TRANSIT: **F streetcar; K, L, and M Muni trains; 24 Muni bus**

The three hilltop parks in this tour are only a few blocks apart, but couldn't be more different. Corona Heights is a rocky outcrop just above the Castro District. Buena Vista Park's densely wooded terrain sprouts unexpectedly from the Haight. Alamo Square is a grassy quadrant amidst classy Victorian houses. All have sweeping views of San Francisco, each offering a unique perspective, but the real pleasure of taking in all three in one shot is in passing through such varied topography within a short space. Wear good shoes for hiking and be prepared to traverse steep, unpaved trails.

● Assuming you've either parked your car or disembarked from public transit down in the Castro, start by climbing from the corner of 16th and Flint streets up to the top of Corona Heights. From just about anywhere along upper Market St., if you look to the west you'll see the red jagged cliff to which we're headed. You can reach park entrances by walking up 16th St. to Flint St., or by walking up Beaver St. above Castro St. Beyond the park entrances, most of the unmarked trails lead to the top, so walk on up. It's a pretty barren hill, with a few trees, grasses, and wildflowers. The most distinctive feature of Corona Heights is the rock itself. The reddish stone is visibly cracking up on the surface, and the trails are strewn with squared off chips and chunks. Pick up a piece and look it over. This rock is chert, formed by plant and animal matter that settled on an ancient seafloor and became petrified before being thrust up here. Similar rock formations turn up elsewhere in the city, but Corona Heights is the most striking example. The hill is crested by dramatic, jagged pinnacles of rock, some of it spray painted on by taggers. From here, take a look around and enjoy a broad view of the city—in addition to the downtown skyline and City Hall, you'll see all of the South of Market area, the Mission, the Castro, Noe Valley, Twin Peaks, and, immediately to the north, Buena Vista Park (our next stop). At lower elevations of Corona Heights are a well-situated playground, the Randall Museum, and a patch of green where people can liberate their dogs from their leashes. The Randall Museum is an educational museum for kids that has a combined emphasis on nature and the arts.

● Descend the trail down to the dog area and exit the park onto Roosevelt Way at Museum Way. Turn right on Roosevelt and bear left onto Park Hill Ave. A block up is Buena Vista Ave., which rings Buena Vista Park. Cross and turn left. The sidewalk here runs around the base of the park's southern slope. Opposite, the large peachy building at 351–355 Buena Vista Ave. East made a brief appearance in Hitchcock's *Vertigo*. Once you're past it, look for a narrow sandy path to the right and follow it up the park's woodsy hillside. It leads to a maze of little spur trails, but try to stay with the widest available trail. This park has long been known as a gay cruising spot after dark. In the '60s, hippies frolicked here as well. Near the top, you'll reach an asphalt path that will serve you well the rest of the way. It winds to good lookout points along the north and east side of the park, and also dips down into a shady gulch that's very sheltered. It's a sweet spot. By now you are surely appreciating the size and varied topography of this inner city park. Buena Vista, originally called Hill Park, was set aside by the city for a park in 1867. Many of the trees were planted on behalf of Adolf Sutro, who annually observed Arbor Day by donating seedlings. John McLaren, who for half a century was superintendent of Golden Gate Park, also over-saw the forestation of Buena Vista Park.

● Find your way toward the western edge of the park. There's an exit near the end of Frederick St. Turn right onto Buena Vista Ave., which curves around the park and leads to Haight St. Along the way, take note of the mansion at No. 737. It was built in 1897 for Richard Spreckels, whose uncle was sugar magnate Claus Spreckels. In the house's early days, writers Ambrose Bierce and Jack London supposedly resided here briefly. More certainly, Graham Nash (whose surname fills this gap: Crosby, Stills, _____, and Young) lived here, as at one time did actor Danny Glover.

● Past Haight St., Yerba Buena Ave. becomes Central Ave. Follow it to the Panhandle, the strip of shaded greenery between Oak and Fell streets. Cross the park to the Fell St. side and turn right. Where the Panhandle ends, turn left at Baker St., then turn right at Hayes St. Alamo Square is three blocks up. Enter midway, about where Pierce St. hits Hayes, and climb up the gentle slope to the top of the park. It's a fairly conventional park, as San Francisco parks go—a hilly lawn with a grove of trees at its center, a single fenced-in tennis court—but the view from the park is a classic. Head over the crest and down the eastern slope and you'll spot the photographers. They're always here, snapping shots of the row of impeccable Victorian houses along Steiner St., with the downtown skyline beyond. It's a surefire cover shot—you'll have seen the image on scores of tourist brochures and guidebooks. The Victorian stars of this view, at 710–722 Steiner, are notable mostly for their near uniformity and for being little changed over the years. They are not the most beautiful Victorians in the city or even on Alamo Square. The house at 1198 Fulton, on the other side of the park, is much more striking but lacks the dramatic backdrop.

● Make your way down to Steiner St. and turn left. While crossing Fulton St. look to the right and you'll see the street descends directly toward City Hall. It's a perfect vantage point for seeing the building's handsome, helmet-like dome. On the opposite corner, at 1000 Fulton, the huge house with the mansard roof is called the Archbishop's Mansion because it was built in 1904 for Archbishop Riordan. It's a classy hotel now, and the Archbishop's old bedroom gets frequent use as a honeymoon suite.

● Continue on Steiner. At No. 1057, on the corner of Golden Gate Ave., the Chateau Tivoli is one of the city's most distinctive buildings. It jabs at the sky with a full complement of

View downtown from Corona Heights

173

turrets and dainty weathervanes, which are the Victorian architectural equivalent of propeller caps. The building has some mighty alluring curves, especially around its bay windows. It was built in 1892 and has served in a variety of capacities, including as a rooming house during the 1960s and '70s. More recently it has been beautifully restored and converted into a hotel (with surprisingly reasonable rates). Walk on around the corner, where the adjacent apartment buildings (at 1409–1417 Golden Gate) are collectively known as the "Seattle Block." The buildings went up at the same time as the Tivoli, and are equally well preserved, and collectively they make a marvelous row.

● Turn left and follow Golden Gate to Divisadero St., where you can grab a refreshment at the Blue Jay Cafe, a lunch and dinner spot that's good for comfort foods and beer. For a less-involved pit stop, head up to the corner of Folsom and snag a table at Cafe Abir, your basic coffeehouse with a laptoppin' crowd. Heading south on Divisadero will get you back to the Castro.

POINTS OF INTEREST

Market and Noe Garage 261 Noe St.

Archbishop's Mansion 1000 Fulton St., 415-563-7872

The Chateau Tivoli 1057 Steiner St., 415-776-5462

Blue Jay Cafe 919 Divisadero St., 415-447-6066

Cafe Abir 1300 Fulton St., 415-567-7654

route summary

1. Start at the base of Corona Heights—at the top of Beaver St. or on the corner of 16th and Flint streets.

2. Follow the trail to the top of Corona Heights.

3. Head down through the dog run, exiting the park at the corner or Museum and Roosevelt St., and head up Roosevelt St.

4. Turn left at Park Hill.

5. At Buena Vista Ave. East, cross to the park and turn left on the sidewalk.

6. Head up the sand-and-wood steps, the first stairway to the right.

7. Find the asphalt path and follow it to the top.

8. Wandering through the park, find your way to the exit near the corner of Buena Vista Ave. West and Frederick St.

9. Turn right on Buena Vista Ave. West.

10. Cross Haight St., and continue on Central Ave.

11. Cross Oak St. to enter the Panhandle and turn right.

12. Turn left at Baker St.

13. Turn right at Hayes St.

14. Enter Alamo Square where Pierce St. meets Hayes St., and head up to the top.

15. Make your way down to Steiner St. and turn left.

16. Turn left at Golden Gate Ave. and follow it to Divisadero St.

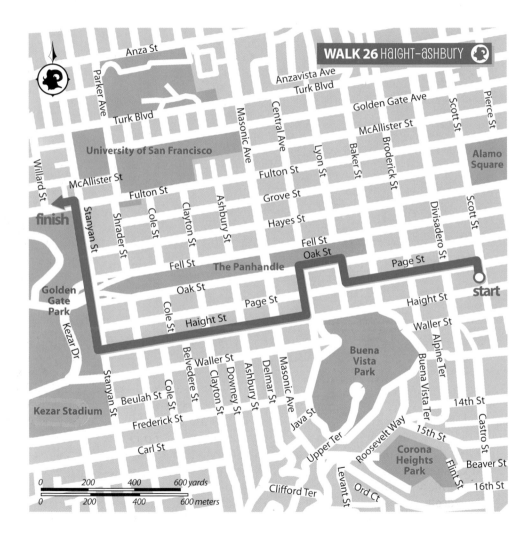

Anza St

Parker Ave

Turk Blvd

University of San Francisco

McAllister St

Willard St

finish

Fulton St

Stanyan St

Shrader St

Cole St

Clayton St

Ashbury St

Masonic Ave

Central Ave

Anzavista Ave
Turk Blvd

Golden Gate Ave

McAllister St

Lyon St

Baker St

Broderick St

Scott St

Pierce St

Alamo
Square

Fulton St

Grove St

Hayes St

Fell St

Oak St

The Panhandle

Divisadero St

Scott St

Page St

start

Golden
Gate
Park

Kezar Dr

Fell St

Oak St

Cole St

Page St

Haight St

Haight St

Waller St

Alpine Ter

Stanyan St

Kezar Stadium

Beulah St

Frederick St

Carl St

Cole St

Belvedere St

Waller St

Clayton St

Downey St

Ashbury St

Delmar St

Masonic Ave

Java St

Buena
Vista
Park

Buena Vista Ter

14th St

Castro St

Upper Ter

Roosevelt Way

15th St

Corona
Heights
Park

Flint St

Beaver St

16th St

Clifford Ter

Levant St

Ord Ct

0   200   400   600 yards

0   200   400   600 meters

26 HaiGHT-aSHBUrY: SaunTerinG BaCK TO THe '60S

BOUNDARIES: **Scott St., Waller St., Fulton St., North Willard St.**
PARKING: **Unrestricted street parking can be found on Oak St., along the Panhandle.**
DISTANCE: **2 miles**
DIFFICULTY: **Easy**
PUBLIC TRANSIT: **24, 71 Muni buses; N Judah streetcar (get off at Duboce Park)**

Along with the Gold Rush, earthquakes, and the Gay '70s, the Summer of Love is one of those things for which San Francisco is commonly known to the outside world. The intersection of Haight and Ashbury streets is the city's most famous crossroads thanks to some craziness that occurred around this nexus from the mid- to late 1960s. While many hippies were simply indulging in the neighborhood's proliferation of drugs and sex, some idealistically saw the "Psychedelic Revolution" as hope for a better world. The neighborhood developed its own economy, spawned its own musical "sound," and acquired a distinctive look, as its residents went for a shaggier, more colorful style than the rest of America. It must have been exciting, mind-blowing, and hilarious. If time travel were possible, Haight St. 1967 would be a tourist mecca. The street today does its best to live up to its reputation. Walking the neighborhood reveals a satisfying blend of historic sites, exquisite Victorian architecture, and bustling alternative commerce.

●   We'll start on a nondescript corner, where Scott and Page streets meet. The building at 250 Scott, where Jack's Record Cellar is located, played a significant role in the neighborhood's countercultural development. The upstairs flat was the home of poet Kenneth Rexroth, a central player in the San Francisco Renaissance. This homegrown literary movement attracted the likes of Jack Kerouac and Allen Ginsberg to San Francisco, bringing the Beat movement to the city by the bay. The cafes of North Beach were where the Beats made the scene, but the serious salons took place in Rexroth's pad. Rexroth distanced himself from the Beats, and moved East, but thousands of students and poets moved into the Haight, looking for cheap rents and an arty bohemian atmosphere in the decade before the hippies. The ground-floor record shop is rarely open, but if it is, step in. It's San Francisco's oldest purveyor of collectible 33-, 45-, and 78-rpm records, and the shop's walls are covered with historic concert posters from legendary jazz, R&B, and rock shows.

- Head west on Page. On the corner of Broderick St., at No. 1090, once stood the Albin Rooming House. According to rock historian Joel Selvin, this apartment building had a "ballroom" in the basement, where Big Brother and the Holding Company and other bands frequently performed. There's nothing to see here, except in your imagination, so keep on truckin'.

- At the corner of Lyon St. turn right. The attractive Victorian at No. 112 was the home of singer Janis Joplin during the Summer of Love. It was an apartment house in those days, and Joplin's room was on the second floor with the curved balcony off the front.

- Head out to Oak St. and cross, turning left, into the Panhandle, a shady, pencil-thin green that's ideal for dog-walking. Exciting events took place here during the '60s, including unforgettable free outdoor concerts. Jimi Hendrix once played here, so as you walk a block west in the park imagine his awesome sound reverberating off the Victorian houses along either side.

- At Central Ave. turn left and at Haight St. turn right. On this block you'll see two relics of the Haight's radical past. The Bound Together Book Collective, at No. 1369, has been peddling anarchist treatises since 1976. Pipe Dreams, at No. 1376, is the oldest extant head shop on the strip. Stop by for an armful of bongs, hookahs, tobacco products, and groovy patches for your torn Levi's.

- At the end of the block, the Magnolia Pub & Brewery is an attractive corner noshery that features its own home-brewed ales. The facade is little changed since the '60s, when the site was the Drogstore Cafe. The name was an obvious appeal to the drug culture, with a twist in the spelling to throw the cops off the scent.

- Across Masonic, Positively Haight Street is a garish grotto of grooviness. The shop deals in everything you'll need for that '60s flashback you've been meaning to have—from tie-dye shirts and incense to loose-fitting imports from India. If none of that's your bag, you can always admire the building's far-out exterior, with its columns shaped like Desi Arnaz congas, and cartoony mural work on the window trim.

- A block up, the corner of Ashbury is the epicenter of the neighborhood. Snap some shots of the crisscrossing Haight and Ashbury street signs and hang a louie. Past Waller St., the Victorian at 710 Ashbury was the home of the Grateful Dead as the band reached its prime (back in the days when bands conveniently lived together, like characters in a TV sitcom). Jerry Garcia, Bob Weir, and Pigpen lived in the psychedelic frat house with managers Rock Scully and Danny Rifkin from 1966 to 1968. Snap a few shots of the house, now home to unfamous millionaires, and beat it on back to Haight.

● Make a left on Ashbury, where half a block up, at 1568 Haight, is Martin Mack's, a standard fake Irish pub. In the late '60s, it was the Pall Mall Lounge, where the "Love Burgers" were very popular, possibly because if you didn't have any scratch you could have yours free of charge. Across the street, at No. 1599, Soul Patch Tattoo and Piercing keeps some of the neighborhood spirit alive. If permanent body art is too much of a commitment, you can get a henna tattoo that'll last a while.

● Past Clayton, at 1665 Haight, the Red Victorian is another standard-bearer for the neighborhood. It's a gorgeous old inn, built in 1904. Inside, it's positively kooky. Owner Sami Sunchild, now well over 70, designed all the guest rooms to induce drug-free hallucinations. She hangs more of her trippy art in a gallery off the lobby, so feel free to have a look inside. The people here are friendly, as is right for a place calling itself a "peace center." Across the street, take a look at Wasteland, a vintage clothing emporium. The Beaux Arts façade is an eyeful.

● The Goodwill store on the corner of Haight and Cole streets was the site of the Straight Theater in 1967 and '68. Legendary shows took place here, and the Dead often used the hall as a rehearsal space. Across the street, at 1775 Haight, a group calling itself the Diggers kept a "crash pad," where anyone needing a free place

Positively Haight Street

to sleep could come. The Diggers provided free food and clothing as well. It
later turned out that actor Peter Coyote
was among the organization's anony-
mous leaders.

- Near Shrader St., Kan Zaman is a way-
out eatery serving Palestinian and
Lebanese food. You can also puff on
a hookah here. The shisha blends are
legal, and likely to make you only a little
dizzy.

- Next block, in a converted bowling alley,
is the immense Amoeba Records, one
of the city's best shopping stops for
music. On many an early evening free,
live shows are held in the store.

- Turn right at Stanyan, walk along the
eastern edge of Golden Gate Park, and
turn left at Fulton. We're looking for the
Jefferson Airplane mansion, at No. 2400.
It's a block up, at the corner of North
Willard, the end of your walk. It's a truly
impressive, three-story manse, with a
neoclassic columned entry. Members of
the band moved here in 1968, painted
the place black, and stayed through the
1970s. Along the way, the Airplane was
converted into a Starship. Singer Grace
Slick left San Francisco for a bigger
galaxy (Los Angeles) in the early '80s,
saying she was tired of being a big fish
in a small pond.

Victorian Detours

While Haight St. is the wigged-out main
stem of the neighborhood, you'd be
missing the flip side of the area's charm
if you didn't take a few short detours to
admire some of San Francisco's finest
residential architecture. You'll find gems
concentrated on the 1700 block of Oak
St. (between Ashbury and Clayton),
the 400 block of Clayton (between
Oak and Page), the 500 block of Cole
(between Page and Haight), and the
1900 block of Page (between Shrader
and Stanyan).

POINTS OF INTEREST

Bound Together Book Collective 1369 Haight St., 415-431-8355

Pipe Dreams 1376 Haight St., 415-431-3553

Magnolia Pub & Brewery 1398 Haight St., 415-864-7468

Positively Haight Street 1400 Haight St., 415-252-8747

Soul Patch Tattoo and Piercing 1599 Haight St., 415-552-3444

Wasteland 1660 Haight, 415-863-3150

Red Victorian B&B 1665 Haight St., 415-864-1978

Kan Zaman 1793 Haight St., 415-751-9656

route summary

1. Start at the corner of Scott and Page streets.
2. Walk west on Page St.
3. Turn right at Lyon St.
4. At Oak St., cross into the Panhandle, and walk west for one block.
5. Turn left at Central Ave.
6. Turn right at Haight St.
7. Turn left at Ashbury St. and walk a block an a half to No. 710, then return to Haight St.
8. Turn left at Haight St.
9. Turn right at Stanyan St.
10. Turn left at Fulton St.
11. Stop at the corner of Fulton and Willard streets.

PACIFIC
OCEAN

China
Beach

Lincoln Park

The Presidio

WALK 27 GOLDEN GATE PARK

Mountain
Lake Park

Clay St

Lake St

California St

Clement St

Geary Blvd

Euclid Ave

Clement St

Geary Blvd

Anza St

Arguello Blvd

Parker Ave

Stanyan St

Balboa St

Cabrillo St

Cabrillo St

Fulton St

Fulton St

Spreckels
Lake

Lloyd
Lake

Golden Gate Park

Stow
Lake

Lily
Pond

start

finish

Polo
Field

Kezar
Stadium

South Dr

Lincoln Way

Carl St

Lincoln Way

Irving St

Irving St

Judah St

Kirkham St

Moraga St

Noriega St

Sunset Blvd

Great Hwy

Ortega St

Pacheco St

Quintara St

Quintara St

0   500   1000   1500 yards

0   500   1000   1500 meters

27 GOLDEN GATE PARK: A LOT OF PARK (AND DANDY MUSEUMS)

BOUNDARIES: **Stanyan St., Fulton St., Lincoln Way, Great Highway**
DISTANCE: **4½ miles**
DIFFICULTY: **Moderate (no great hills, but it's a long, indirect route through a huge park)**
PARKING: **Street parking is easier to find on weekdays than on weekends. The underground lot by the De Young Museum is reached via the 8th Ave. entrance, on the north side of the park.**
PUBLIC TRANSIT: **N Judah streetcar; 6, 7, and 71 Muni buses**

Golden Gate Park is a celebration of nature—only, there is really nothing natural about it. The 1,000-acre urban parkland, among the nation's largest, is a series of groves, gardens, and lakes, all seeded, shaped, and constructed by human hands and machinery. When the city set aside the land, in 1870, it was a windswept expanse of sand and shrubs that few thought could be tamed for the leisurely enjoyment of the local citizenry. William Hammond Hall, the park's surveyor and first superintendent, planted barley, and then lupine, both of which rooted and spread across the sand, holding it down and making it possible for further planting to take place. Within ten years, natural-looking woodlands had been established across the once-barren landscape. The park also has historic buildings, museums, a boathouse, a bison paddock, and a classy brewpub. Plan on spending a few hours walking and exploring the terrain before enjoying a well-earned beer or meal.

● Start at McLaren Lodge, near the convergence of Stanyan St. and John F. Kennedy Dr. This lodge-like graystone, with Moorish-Gothic overtones, was built in 1896 and serves as the park's headquarters (but it offers only limited information to visitors). It is named for John McLaren, who served as park superintendent from 1890 until 1947—an astonishing run of 57 years that ended with McLaren's death at age 97. Clearly, the guy was as sturdy as an ox.

● Follow JFK Dr. into the park, and on the right-hand side you'll soon see the Conservatory of Flowers, a grand glass house constructed in 1876. It's the oldest structure in the park. Making a brief visit is well worth the $5 admission charge. The humid interior is a welcome contrast with the park's typical blustery weather, making the conservatory a suitable home for the varied and exotic tropical plants housed within.

- From the Conservatory, cross JFK and look for the 20-foot-tall ferns. Follow the dirt path through this Jurassic-looking grove, veering left at the fork. You'll quickly reach secluded Lily Pond, which the trail loops partway around as it leads to Middle Dr. East. See if you can spot the unofficial trails leading to hidden homeless camps within some of the dense growth here and in other parts of the park.

- Cross Middle Dr. East and turn left (east), looking for the entrance to the National AIDS Memorial Grove. Designated by an Act of Congress, the grove is a reflective place where people can think of loved ones lost to AIDS. Memorial services are often held here, and a stone patio along the path, called Circle of Friends, has names of some victims of the disease etched in an ever-widening spiral. From there, the path runs past a stand of young redwoods and through a grassy dell and alongside an artfully landscaped dry creek. Past that, by a meditative circle, look for stone steps to the left and head up. When you reach the asphalt path, veer left, then right where a dirt path heads downhill. (This should all be fairly easy to follow when you're actually on the trail.) Sticking to the main path downhill will get you through a stone garden, and then a baseball field will come into view. Veer back toward Middle Dr. East and turn left.

- Veer right at Martin Luther King Jr. Dr. When you see the sign for the Shakespeare Garden, follow it, and you'll soon reach the Music Concourse; turn right. Here you'll see the new California Academy of Sciences, the recently reopened De Young Museum, the huge band shell called the Temple of Music, and the Japanese Tea Garden. Walk through the concourse.

- The concourse area was laid out for the 1894 Midwinter International Exposition, commonly described as a chintzy flop, but looking pretty interesting if photographs from the time are any indication. Some 200 temporary structures filled the grounds, many of them reflecting the pretentious and exotic tastes of San Franciscans at the time. The city was eager to make a big impression on more established bigwigs of the East Coast and Chicago.

- In any case, all that survives from the Expo is the Japanese Village, now called the Japanese Tea Garden. After the Expo, stewardship of the gardens was turned over to Makoto Hagiwara, who built a house on the grounds and lived here with his family. Hagiwara was fired in 1900, rehired in 1907 and stayed on until he was interned along with thousands of Japanese immigrants during World War II. Hagiwara's other contribution to the local culture was the introduction of fortune cookies (invented by his cook in 1914), which were originally made as a unique snack to serve at the Tea Garden but are now ubiquitous in Chinese restaurants.

- The new De Young Museum opened in 2005, initially to mixed reviews that have warmed since. San Franciscans are always a little suspicious of modern architecture, especially bold designs like this one, with its askew, 144-foot tower prominent above the park's treetops. It's clad in unprotected copper, which has quickly begun acquiring a patina that's very easy on the eyes. Admission is $10, which deters quick in-and-out visits. The De Young's art collection and exhibits warrant a follow-up trip, so let's keep walking.

- Turn left on Hagiwara Tea Garden Dr. and walk back out to MLK, cross the street, and enter the Strybing Arboretum via the Friend Gate. The arboretum is another site worth a dedicated visit, comprising 70 acres showcasing some 7,500 varieties of plants from around the world. Its labyrinth of paths are tempting to get lost in. For the purpose of our westward trek, take every right turn and you'll end up at an exit a little ways farther down MLK.

- Just outside the arboretum, look across the street for stone steps, which lead to Stow Lake, and head up. At the top of the steps, turn

The Conservatory of Flowers

left on the shaded path, which clings to the water's edge. The lake here is a narrow ring, looking like a calm stream looped around high Strawberry Hill. You'll see plenty of paddle boats and ducks. When you reach the rustic stone bridge, cross and turn right, following the inside of the curvature of the lake. Soon after you pass the Chinese Pavilion, looking like a gazebo awaiting a tea party, you'll hear and then see Huntington Falls, a charming artifice. This is perhaps the only part of the park where the hush of city traffic is completely drowned out, making it worth pausing for a little break here. Continue along the trail to Roman Bridge, cross it, and head left toward the boathouse. Behind the boathouse a trail leads to JFK Dr. Turn left.

● After crossing Cross Over Dr. and Transverse Dr., look for the footpath to the left of JFK. You'll be walking past a wooded area to the left, and picnic grounds and large green meadows to the right. Speedway Meadow has been the site of many an outdoor concert, including the immensely popular Hardly Strictly Bluegrass Festival, which takes place every October. The trail leads to the Polo Field, which is surrounded by a "trotting track" for equestrians. Golden Gate Park Stables are across the Polo Field. The field is not so much known for polo matches as it is for the cultural events that have taken place here. On the afternoon of January 14, 1967, the "Summer of Love" got off to an early start here, with the Gathering of the Tribes and Human Be-In. Some 30,000 hippies congregated here to hear Timothy Leary's call to "Turn on, tune in, drop out." Allen Ginsberg ranted, the Grateful Dead jammed, and the crowd tripped late into the night. When the Dead's Jerry Garcia died in August 1995, a spontaneous gathering took place in the Polo Field as fans instinctively came here to remember the keeper of the '60s flame.

● Beyond the stables, a path leads back to JFK Dr., where you turn left. On the other side, you'll see the Bison Paddock. Golden Gate Park has no zoo and is more about flora than fauna, but a herd of buffalo has lived here since 1892.

● Follow JFK around the golf course. Before the street ends at the Great Highway, the Dutch Windmill overlooks a garden of tulips. The windmill was built in 1902 to pump water into the park. It was restored in the early 1980s and still works. There's another windmill at the southwest corner of the park, but it's in a sad state of disrepair.

● The Beach Chalet stands at the corner of JFK and the Great Highway. Designed by Willis Polk, the restaurant opened in 1925. The downstairs lobby is covered with murals, painted in 1936 by French-born artist Lucien Labaudt. Upstairs, in a room dominated by plate-glass windows facing the ocean, the microbrewery is a lively spot for breakfast, lunch, or dinner. The beer is good, and on many evenings live jazz combos perform.

POINTS OF INTEREST

Conservatory of Flowers John F. Kennedy Dr., 415-666-7001

Hagiwara Japanese Tea Garden Hagiwara Tea Garden Dr., 415-831-2700

M.H. De Young Memorial Museum 50 Hagiwara Tea Garden Dr., 415-863-3330

Strybing Arboretum & Botanical Gardens 9th Ave. at Lincoln Way, 415-661-1316

Beach Chalet 1000 Great Highway, 415-386-8439

route summary

1. Begin at the John McLaren Lodge, at the intersection of Stanyan St. and John F. Kennedy Dr.
2. Follow JFK Dr. to the Conservatory of Flowers.
3. Opposite the Conservatory, follow the dirt trail through the fern grove.
4. Follow the trail halfway around Lily Pond.
5. Where the trail hits Middle Dr. East, turn left.
6. At Middle Dr. and Bowling Green Dr., enter the AIDS Memorial Grove.
7. Follow the path through the AIDS Memorial Grove.
8. A series of dirt and asphalt paths will lead to the ball field. If you get lost, just follow Middle Dr. East in a westerly direction.
9. At Martin Luther King Jr. Dr., turn right.
10. Past the Shakespeare Garden, turn right at the entry to the Music Concourse and walk through it, to Hagiwara Tea Garden Dr.
11. Turn left at Tea Garden Dr. to return to MLK Dr.
12. Across MLK, enter the Strybing Arboretum and turn right.
13. In the arboretum, veer right where trails meet and you'll end up farther up MLK Dr.
14. Cross MLK Dr. and head up the stone steps to Stow Lake.
15. Turn left onto the trail.
16. Cross Rustic Bridge and turn right.
17. Cross Roman Bridge and turn left.
18. Behind the boathouse follow the trail to JFK Dr. and turn left.
19. Past Transverse Dr. get on the footpath and follow it past Speedway Meadow, all the way to the Polo Field.
20. Loop partway around the Polo Field (or diagonally across it) to the stables.
21. Behind the stables, find your way back to JFK Dr. and turn left.
22. Follow JFK Dr. as it bends in a northwest direction, all the way to the Beach Chalet.

Fern Grove

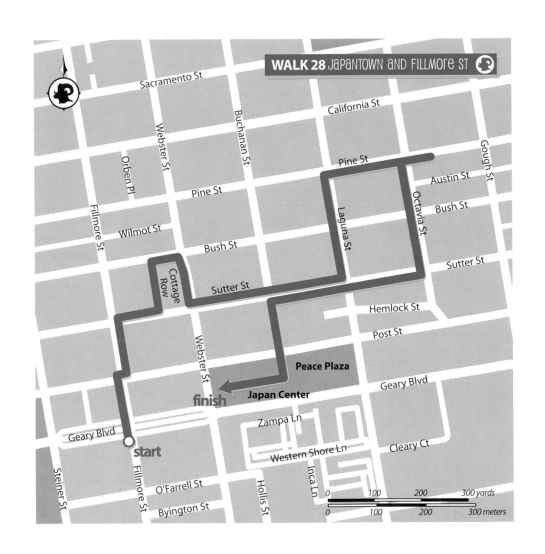

Sacramento St

California St

Pine St

Austin St

Gough St

Webster St

Buchanan St

Pine St

Laguna St

Octavia St

Bush St

Orben Pl

Fillmore St

Wilmot St

Bush St

Sutter St

Sutter St

Cottage Row

Sutter St

Hemlock St

Post St

Webster St

Peace Plaza

Japan Center

Geary Blvd

finish

Geary Blvd

Zampa Ln

start

Fillmore St

Western Shore Ln

Cleary Ct

Steiner St

O'Farrell St

Hollis St

Inca Ln

Byington St

0   100   200   300 yards

0   100   200   300 meters

28 Japantown and Fillmore Street: Where Buddhist Temples and Blues Bars Meet

BOUNDARIES: **Fillmore St., Geary Blvd., Pine St., Octavia St.**
DISTANCE: **1¼ miles**
DIFFICULTY: **Easy**
PARKING: **There is a lot beneath Japan Center. Street parking is often available on Webster St., south of Geary Blvd.**
PUBLIC TRANSIT: **The 22 and 38 Muni buses stop at the corner of Geary Blvd. and Fillmore St.**

Japantown is an odd and interesting neighborhood. Japanese immigrants began settling here after the '06 quake, and were unjustly moved from their homes and placed in internment camps during World War II. The African Americans who moved in were drawn by jobs in wartime industries, but 1960s redevelopment of the area caused yet another exodus as a sizeable proportion of the neighborhood's housing was demolished to make way for the widened Geary Blvd. Expressway and for hotels and retail structures. Although the Japanese had dispersed by that time, the redevelopment included construction of Japan Center, along with some senior housing catering to elderly Japanese. So what we have here is a modern commercial district with a strong Japanese flavor and only a very small remnant of the Japanese community. Similarly, Fillmore St. retains hints of the area's African American past. Amid the modern hotels and condominiums are some gorgeous Victorians that were spared the mid-century wrecking ball. The neighborhood is pleasant for walking, but the chief interest here is obviously inside Japan Center itself. We'll end up there.

● Start at the southwest corner of Geary Blvd. and Fillmore St., at the Fillmore Auditorium, legendary for its rock shows during the 1960s. The elegant hall predates rock and roll by several decades, however. It was built in 1912 and was originally dubbed the Majestic Ball Room. Very likely some of the most remarkable shows to ever take place in the building were by jazz and R&B performers during the heyday of the black Fillmore District. Count Basie, Billie Holliday, and a young James Brown electrified audiences here. Rock promoter Bill Graham put on shows here from 1966 to 1968. All the local bands (Dead, Airplane, Holding Company) took the stage on a regular basis, and out-of-town guests included Jimi Hendrix, the Doors, and the Velvet

Underground. The Fillmore re-emerged as one of the city's preeminent rock venues in the 1990s and remains an intimate music hall where top-tier talent performs in a variety of musical styles.

- Cross Geary Blvd. to reach the Boom Boom Room, a Fillmore District stalwart. This classy little cinderblock dive was for many years known as Jack's. It's a lounge-like, inner-city juke, with a checkered linoleum floor, padded booths, and a small stage where blues artists perform nightly. During the late 1990s, the club was partly owned by bluesman John Lee Hooker, who for many years lived in Redwood City, just south of San Francisco. Hooker died in 2001.

- Cross Fillmore St. at Post St. On the ground floor of the purple Victorian at No. 1712, Marcus Books specializes in literature by black writers. The house itself was moved here during the 1960s, as were many other homes during the redevelopment of the neighborhood. In its earlier location, on Post St. where the Buchanan St. Mall is now, this house was home to Jimbo's Bop City, a music locus in the old Fillmore where the likes of Charlie Parker joined in after-hours jams.

- Turn right on Sutter St. and walk on the north (right-hand) side of the street. Before reaching Webster St., head left up the path called Cottage Row. The six two-story cottages along this little pedestrian block were built in 1882. Cottage Row ends at Bush St. Turn right and right again on Webster. At No. 1737, the John J. Vollmer House is one of the neighborhood's better surviving Victorians. Built in 1885, it was moved here in the mid-1970s. It was evidently a tight fit—part of the house had to be sliced off to get it into the narrow lot. Nevertheless, the trim, with flowers carved into the woodwork, is some of the city's finest.

- Turn left on Sutter and left on Laguna St. At 1909 Bush St. is the Konko Church, where members of a sect of the Shinto religion worship. The church, built in a simple yet graceful Japanese style, went up in 1973.

- Turn right on Pine St. Just off the corner of Octavia St., at 1881 Pine, the large structure with the stupa on the roof is home of the Buddhist Church. The temple was built in 1937, but the Jodo Shinshu congregation began worshipping here, in an earlier building, in 1914. Hidden within the stupa are relics of the Buddha, given to the congregation by the Emperor of Thailand in 1935.

- Turn right on Octavia. At the corner of Bush, Quince is an intimate Italian-French restaurant that's worth knowing about. Chef Michael Tusk's cuisine draws raves. It's open for dinner only. Across Bush, the corner lot behind the row of eucalyptus trees on the Octavia St. side is of historical interest. Mary Ellen Pleasant, known widely as "Mammy," built her house here. From 1852 until her death in 1904, Pleasant caused quite a stir in San Francisco more or less by being a black woman who enjoyed tremendous success here. From surviving photos, she appears to have been a very serious and intelligent woman who probably took no guff from anyone. The house she built here became known as the "House of Mystery," after her business partner and assumed lover Thomas Bell died in it under mysterious circumstances. Local papers never seemed to know how to deal with this woman, and generally implied she was a voodoo priestess of some kind. In fact, she was from Philadelphia and for decades aided slaves escaping via the Underground Railroad. Even in San Francisco she often harbored black fugitives, all the while amassing her fortune by operating a string of well-regarded boarding houses and investing in the stock market and real estate. Her mansion was destroyed in 1927. There's a plaque imbedded in the sidewalk, amid the eucalyptus trees.

- Continue on Octavia and turn right on Sutter St. At Buchanan turn left into the Buchanan St. Mall, a pedestrian shopping strip that echoes the Asian emphasis of Japan Center, to which the street directly leads. Japan Center was built in the 1960s, and architecturally it reflects the simple taste of the era but with distinct Japanese overtones. It was designed

Peace Pagoda, Japan Center

by Minoru Yamasaki, who went on to achieve greater heights by designing the ill-fated World Trade Center in New York. A 100-foot pagoda stands in Peace Plaza, a stark concrete slab where the elderly sometimes take in some sun. To the left is the Miyako Hotel, a very fashionable hostelry in which the rooms have sleek Japanese stylings. To the right is Kintetsu Mall. Go on in.

● The mall has the meandering feel of an airport, with food courts and narrow stores selling the same sorts of cultural curios you'd find in duty-free shops. If the impulse strikes you, you might wind up with a new silk kimono while here. Of more likely interest is the Kinokuniya Bookstore, where several aisles are devoted to Japanese art books, Manga comics, DVDs of anime films, and a smattering of Godzilla classics. On your way there, you'll pass through the restaurant mall, where the decor really lays it on with the movie-set Japantown feel. The windows all have artfully arranged plastic meals on display to lure you in. Mifune is a good spot for a bowl of hot udon soup. The mall also has several cafes and karaoke bars, if you're planning on hanging out awhile. Downstairs, accessible via Post St. near the corner of Webster, be sure to drop by the Nijiya Market, a supermarket in miniature, with tiny carts and narrow aisles stocked with Japanese foodstuffs. Just past the registers, an aisle is stocked with a huge selection of bento lunches neatly packed in plastic trays.

POINTS OF INTEREST

Fillmore Auditorium 1805 Geary Blvd., 415-346-6000

Boom Boom Room 1601 Fillmore St., 415-673-8000

Marcus Books 1712 Fillmore St., 415-346-4222

Konko Kyo Church 1909 Bush St.

Buddhist Church 1881 Pine St.

Quince Restaurant 1701 Octavia St., 415-775-8500

Miyako Hotel 1625 Post St., 415-922-3200

Kinokuniya Bookstore 1581 Webster St., 415-567-7625

Nijiya Market 1737 Post St., 415-563-1901

route summary

1. Start at the Fillmore Auditorium on the southwest corner of Geary Blvd. and Fillmore St.
2. Proceed north on Fillmore St.
3. Turn right on Sutter St. and walk half a block on the north side of the street.
4. Turn left on Cottage Row (pedestrian street).
5. Turn right on Bush St.
6. Turn right on Webster St.
7. Turn left on Sutter St.
8. Turn left on Laguna St.
9. Turn right on Pine St.
10. Turn right on Octavia St.
11. Turn right on Sutter St.
12. Turn left on Buchanan St. (pedestrian mall).
13. Cross Post St. to Peace Plaza.
14. To the right, enter Kintestu Mall.

The Presidio

Lincoln Blvd

Hays

Mountain Lake

Mountain Lake Park

Pacific Ave

Lake St

5th Ave

4th Ave

3rd Ave

Arguello Blvd

Cornwall St

21st Ave

20th Ave

19th Ave

Lake St

14th Ave

Funston Ave

12th Ave

11th Ave

10th Ave

California St

Clement St

start

24th Ave

23rd Ave

18th Ave

17th Ave

16th Ave

15th Ave

Clement St

5th Ave

4th Ave

3rd Ave

2nd Ave

Arguello Blvd

finish

Geary Blvd

Funston Ave

Park Presidio

8th Ave

7th Ave

6th Ave

Anza St

Anza St

Balboa St

25th Ave

24th Ave

23rd Ave

22nd Ave

Balboa St

18th Ave

17th Ave

16th Ave

14th Ave

12th Ave

11th Ave

10th Ave

9th Ave

Cabrillo St

Cabrillo St

Fulton St

Golden Gate Park

| 0 | 200 | 400 | 600 yards |
| 0 | 200 | 400 | 600 meters |

29 richmond district: an international stroll

BOUNDARIES: **Arguello St., Clement St., Geary Blvd., 25th Ave.**
DISTANCE: **1½ miles**
DIFFICULTY: **Easy**
PARKING: **Street parking is metered, with two-hour limits. Parking is very difficult to find on the weekend.**
PUBLIC TRANSIT: **1 and 38 Muni buses**

Clement St. in the Inner Richmond District will always be "New Chinatown," even though Chinese immigrants have operated businesses here since the 1970s. The area naturally invites contrast to the old Chinatown, and indeed there are interesting similarities and differences. Being out in San Francisco's Fog Belt, the Richmond has always attracted more than its share of immigrants, and there's plenty of evidence of many waves of newcomers, some of whom are obviously still here. To be sure, along Clement you'll find roasted ducks hanging in windows, along with steamed pork buns, produce stalls, and bargain bazaars to rival if not surpass those of the old Chinatown. But in the mix you'll also encounter the city's best used bookstore, Russian tearooms, Korean barbecue joints, Irish bars, bohemian cafes, and loads of Southeast Asian restaurants. This walk is sort of an eating and shopping excursion that needn't involve maxing out your credit card. The main idea is to snoop around a bit to see what sorts of intriguing items you might find along some of the city's more interesting streets.

● Begin at the end of Clement St., on the corner of Arguello Blvd., and go west. If the fog is blowing the other way, you'll know you're headed in the right direction. If it's daytime the Plough and the Stars, at No. 116, will not be open, which is just as well as we've only just started our walk. Note that this is no fake Irish pub, which should be apparent from the bar's exterior, which doesn't bother to project a St. Paddy's shamrock image. Irish musicians perform here every night, and many of the patrons come to do a little fancy steppin'.

● A block up, at No. 208, is Minh's Garden, where perfectly passable Vietnamese food is served. Better yet, on the next block, at No. 309, is Burma Super Star. Despite the Hollywood leanings of its name, Burma Super Star is a fairly humble place that serves a type of cuisine not commonly found around the U.S. The food of Myanmar

Back Story: The San Francisco Columbarium

While exploring Clement St. in the Inner Richmond District, it's worth a quick detour to check out the San Francisco Columbarium. It's one of those places San Franciscans have heard about but never get around to visiting, and it's just a couple of blocks from where this tour begins.

A columbarium is a building divided into compartments in which the ashes of the dead can be kept. The word derives from the Latin columba, meaning "dove," and is a reference to the tightly arranged coops built for domesticated doves and pigeons. That's not particularly flattering. It might also be appropriate to think of columbaria as old folks' homes for folks who are just a wee bit beyond old. The San Francisco Columbarium, built in 1898, is a particularly elegant example. It's a gorgeous piece of historic architecture with beautiful tiling and graceful glass enclosures rising three stories above the main floor.

San Francisco is a city nearly devoid of cemeteries. Only two graveyards remain in the city—in the Presidio and behind the Mission Dolores. Large cemeteries formerly covered much of the Inner Richmond, and the Columbarium was within the 167-acre Odd Fellows Cemetery. During the early 20th century all of these graveyards were moved south of San Francisco to the strange city of Colma, where the dead vastly outnumber the living. Thus, for the most part, San Francisco keeps the dearly departed at arm's length. The Columbarium was spared, even though cremation was for several decades outlawed in the city. It was restored in the late 1970s.

The Columbarium is the only place within the city limits where a civilian can hope to rest in peace. Vaults are privately owned, and can be bought and sold much like real estate. The value of vaults rises and falls (mostly rises) with more energy than San Francisco's skyrocketing housing market. Annually, the Columbarium throws a cocktail party for people who own but do not yet occupy vaults. It's a way for future neighbors to get to know each other before they meet their makers.

The Columbarium is just a few blocks from Clement and Arguello. On Arguello walk two blocks south, past Geary, and turn left onto Anza St. Turn left onto Loraine Court, a cul-de-sac that ends at the entrance to the Columbarium.

is spicy and aromatic, with rich curries and sizzling vegetables bringing together the influences of both east and south Asia. Sure enough, this little joint is very popular.

- On the next corner, Toy Boat Dessert Cafe is an ice cream parlor. While you're waiting for your server to scrape those scoops for you, check out the store's amusing array of toys and novelty items. They still sell Pez dispensers and Peewee Herman dolls here.

- Enough food. Kamei, at No. 547, takes up two buildings, each filled to the rafters with restaurant and kitchen supplies. The aisles contain neatly arranged stacks of knives, bamboo placemats, chopsticks "for special guests," soup bowls, rice bowls, clay pots, and teapots.

- Across the street, Green Apple is a large emporium of used books. It's a densely packed series of rooms both upstairs and down, with additional space a little ways up the block. Some patrons have been known to simply disappear here, never to be seen again.

- New May Wah Supermarket, at No. 719, is the kind of place you expect to find in a Chinatown-type of environment. It has an endless aisle devoted to Asian snacks—shrimp puffs, Pocky Sticks, and the like—and other rows fully stocked with bean sauces, fish sauces, and canned tropical fruits of the sort that aren't grown in the States (rambutan, longans, lychees, etc.). Take a gander.

- Wander out past Park Presidio Blvd. and you're committing yourself to a fairly long walk (unless you hop on a No. 38 bus for the return trip). Make a left on Park Presidio, cut over to Geary Blvd., and follow it all the way out to 25th Ave., and you might find

Kamei on Clement St.

yourself wanting to move out this way. Places you ought to look out for are Kabuto Sushi, at 5121 Geary, which sometimes gets singled out as the city's best sushi restaurant. A few blocks farther, Ton Kiang, at No. 5821, prepares outstanding dim sum in an unfrenzied atmosphere (you select your dim sum from a menu, and it is prepared to order). Tommy's Mexican Restaurant, at No. 5929, is as well known for its margaritas as it is for its fine Yucatecan cuisine. The drinks are prepared by hand (no mixes) with high-quality tequila and fresh ingredients. The food goes down mighty easy after one or two of 'em.

● Tiki bars are all the rage around the Bay Area these days. They're throwbacks to the 1930s, when mainlanders first discovered ukulele music and longed for the easy life under South Seas palms. Trad'r Sam, at No. 6150, is no throwback. It's been operating out here in the fog since before WWII. It has all the atmosphere of Mr. and Mrs. Howell's hut, and fruity drinks prepared by hard-working barkeeps resemble Carmen Miranda's hats. Show up in the afternoon if you want to avoid the just-turned-21 crowd.

POINTS OF INTEREST

Plough and the Stars 116 Clement St., 415-751-1122

Minh's Garden 208 Clement St., 415-751-8211

Burma Super Star 309 Clement St., 415-387-2147.

Toy Boat Dessert Cafe 401 Clement St., 415-751-7505

Kamei 525-547 Clement St., 415-666-3688

Green Apple Books and Music 506 Clement St., 415-387-2272

New May Wah Supermarket 719 Clement St., 415-221-9826

Kabuto Sushi 5121 Geary Blvd., 415-752-5652

Ton Kiang 5821 Geary Blvd., 415-386-8530

Trad'r Sam 6150 Geary Blvd., 415-221-0773

Tommy's Mexican Restaurant 5929 Geary Blvd., 415-387-4747

San Francisco Columbarium 1 Loraine Court

route summary

1.   Start at the Arguello Blvd. end of Clement St. and proceed west.
2.   Turn left at Park Presidio Blvd.
3.   Turn right at Geary Blvd.

Toy Boat Dessert Cafe

30 LANDS END: CLIFFSIDE PARKS ON THE EDGE

BOUNDARIES: 48th Ave., Geary St., and the edge of the continent
DISTANCE: 3 miles
DIFFICULTY: Strenuous (a bit hazardous in spots)
PARKING: Street parking on 48th Ave. near the end of Geary or Anza, has no time limit.
PUBLIC TRANSIT: 38 Muni bus

San Francisco is oriented toward its bay, but to overlook the coastal trails that run along the cliffs at the city's western edge is to miss out on some very striking natural scenery. Trails, some of them slim and rocky footpaths, crook down to secluded beaches and back up to landmark buildings such as the Cliff House and the Palace of the Legion of Honor. The area's intriguing history manifests itself in captivating ways. The washed-out remnants of the Sutro Baths are a modern ruin looking much like the leavings of a long-gone civilization. Be aware that nudity is permitted on some of the beaches, so the natural scenery you encounter along the more secluded trails may include humans in their birthday suits. Take this walk on a cold day if you want to avoid such surprises.

- Begin at Sutro Heights Park, where once stood the estate of Adolf Sutro (see box). Sutro was an unusually civic-minded millionaire, who fashioned his gardens into a grand park open to the public. He had the grounds landscaped in the style of an Italian garden, and although some cracked wise about Sutro's unrefined taste in art, San Franciscans seldom objected to the plaster nymph statues that peered out between the trees and shrubbery. All is gone now, save for some cypress trees, lovely rolling lawns, and what appears to be the broken footprint of Sutro's old manor house, which fell into disrepair after his death and was demolished in 1939. Beside a little gazebo-like structure, take the path that leads down to Point Lobos Ave. and the seaside cliffs.

- Cross the street and make your way down to the Cliff House. There have been several Cliff Houses on this site, beginning in 1863. The first Cliff House was owned by a retired sea captain known as Pop Foster, and for a time, Foster's Cliff House was known as a house of ill repute. Adolf Sutro bought the remote resort in the 1890s, it burned down in 1894, and Sutro had it rebuilt two years later. The Sutro Cliff House was the magnificent, cliff-hanging Victorian beauty so often featured in historic photos. Unfortunately, the most familiar of those photos is the 1907 shot of the building going up in flames. The current Cliff House, completed in 1909, is much less comely from the street but after a recent remodel has become a fine-looking restaurant and bistro, with exotic *Casablanca* decor and picture windows making the most of the sea view. If you're not eating, walk on through, find your way to the veranda overlooking the cliffs, and maybe plop some coins into the Camera Obscura for a large 360-degree view of the scenery. The big camera is mostly remarkable as a relic of archaic technology. The Camera Obscura represents a link in the chain of inventions that led to photography; Leonardo da Vinci drew up plans for such a device in the 15th century. Part of the scenery conveyed by the camera's lens includes Seal Rocks, where sea lions have long basked. Their numbers have dwindled in recent years, though, as the sea lions have migrated into the bay, where they laze about on the boat docks of Pier 39.

● Back out on the sidewalk, head north, to Louis' Restaurant. It's a casual and friendly diner with the same exceptional views you'd enjoy at the much more expensive Cliff House.

Back Story: Adolph Sutro

Adolf Sutro (1830-1898), a native of Prussia, moved to San Francisco during the Gold Rush and made his fortune on the Comstock Lode. He was an engineer, and his ticket to glory was in developing a tunnel that drained and ventilated the deep silver mines around Virginia City, Nevada. When Sutro sold his tunnel in 1879, he turned his attention to real estate in the rapidly growing city of San Francisco. He bought nearly 10 percent of the land within the city limits, most of it undeveloped at the time. Sutro served one term as the city's mayor, from 1894 to 1898. He termed himself the "anti-octopus" candidate, referring to the power of the Southern Pacific Railroad, which at the time was a many-tentacled political force.

● Next to Louis', a trail leads down to the Sutro Baths, one of San Francisco's more fascinating historic sites. Walk all the way down into the cove where long-abandoned swimming pools have become desolate duck ponds. You'll have to use your imagination (and refer to more old photos) to get an idea how awesome the Sutro Baths were. While walking (carefully) among the ruins, see if you can picture massive steel framework supporting a glass dome overhead, with several large pools, slides, three restaurants, and a grandstand that seated 3,700. The water in each pool was of a different temperature, and some pools contained salt water while others had fresh water. The baths were exceedingly popular for awhile, but by the late 1930s attendance had declined and the facility was converted into an ice rink. It closed in 1952 and burned down in 1966. (Lots of fires around these parts.) Make your way back up to the street. At the top of the steps turn left and walk through the parking lot to the Coastal Trail. We'll follow a small portion of the Coastal Trail, which stretches up and down the state of California. Here, the trail hems fairly closely to the cliffs, overlooking the rocks and surf below. During low tide you can see the remains of three shipwrecks. If some parts of the trail pass through cleared land, it's due to a GGNRA program that is removing nonnative plants in order to encourage a return of native species.

● The trail skirts the western edge of Lincoln Park; a few hundred yards up, a spur leads right to the Palace of the Legion of Honor, one of the city's biggest art museums. Intriguingly, the building is a replica of a replica. The 1915 Panama Pacific Exposition included a French Pavilion, modeled on the Palais de la Légion d'Honneur in Paris. The French Pavilion showcased French art during the expo, then was torn down afterwards. Alma Spreckels,

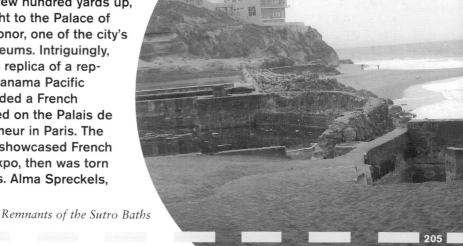

Remnants of the Sutro Baths

wife of sugar magnate Adolf Spreckels, missed the pavilion and had this more per-manent version built. It opened in 1924. The museum's holdings include many 20th-century European masterpieces. You don't need to enter to have a look at Rodin's *The Thinker,* in front. It's a bronze cast, but Rodin oversaw its production. Some memo-rable scenes from Hitchcock's *Vertigo* were shot here.

● If it's nice weather, you can opt to hit a couple of beaches rather than visit the museum. To get to China Beach, take the Coastal Trail to McLaren Ave. and into the Richmond District. Follow it as it curves to the left and then hits Sea Cliff. You'll see some steps leading down to the beach. China Beach, so named for the camp of Chinese fishermen based here prior to the '06 quake, has swimmable surf, if you can stand the cold tem-peratures.

● Farther down Sea Cliff, where the street ends, a footpath (actually, a continuation of the Coastal Trail) leads into the Presidio and to Baker Beach. This is the city's prime sunbathing spot, with a spectacular view of the sea, the Golden Gate, and the bridge. Swimming is not advisable, due to dangerous riptides. From here you can walk the sands almost all the way to the Golden Gate Bridge.

POINTS OF INTEREST

Cliff House 1090 Point Lobos Ave., 415-386-3330

Louis' Restaurant 902 Point Lobos Ave., 415-387-6330

Palace of the Legion of Honor Lincoln Park, 34th Ave. and Clement St., 415-863-3330

route summary

1. Start at Sutro Heights Park.
2. Walk down the path to Point Lobos Ave. and cross to the Cliff House.
3. From the Cliff House, go north, back up Point Lobos Ave., and head down the trail to the Sutro Baths.
4. From the Sutro Baths, return to the street and turn left, into the parking lot.
5. At the end of the parking lot, continue down the Coastal Trail.
6. A few hundred yards up the trail, turn right into Lincoln Park and the Palace of the Legion of Honor.
7. Return to the Coastal Trail and continue all the way until the trail meets McLaren Ave.
8. Follow McLaren Ave. as it curves left; where it meets Sea Cliff Ave., turn down the trail to China Beach.
9. From China Beach, take the trail back up to Sea Cliff Ave. and turn left.
10. At the end of Sea Cliff Ave. follow the trail down to Baker Beach.

Appendix 1: WaLKS BY THeMe

architecture

Financial District (Walk 3)
Nob Hill (Walk 10)
Pacific Heights (Walk 17)

arts & culture

Union Square (Walk 4)
Civic Center (Walk 12)
Embarcadero South (Walk 18)
Yerba Buena Gardens (Walk 19)
Mission Murals (Walk 21)

DINING, SHOPPING & entertainment

North Beach (Walk 7)
North Beach Bars (Walk 8)
Tenderloin (Walk 13)
Mission Bars (Walk 22)
Castro (Walk 24)
Japantown (Walk 28)
Richmond (Walk 29)
Haight (Walk 26)

HISTOrY

Lower Market St. (Walk 1)
Jackson Square: Barbary Coast (Walk 6)

UrBaN ParKS

Marina (Walk 15)
Presidio (Walk 16)
Bernal Heights (Walk 23)
Corona Heights & Buena Vista Park (Walk 25)
Golden Gate Park (Walk 27)
Lands End (Walk 30)

STairways

Telegraph Hill (Walk 9)
Russian Hill (Walk 11)

Appendix 2: POINTS OF INTEREST

FOOD & DRINK

Absinthe Brasserie and Bar 398 Hayes St., 415-551-1590
Balboa Cafe 3199 Fillmore St., 415-921-3944
Beach Chalet 1000 Great Highway, 415-386-8439
Bechelli's 2346 Chestnut St., 415-346-1801
Bix 56 Gold St., 415-433-6300
Blue Jay Cafe 919 Divisadero St., 415-447-6066
Boudin Bakery 160 Jefferson St., 415-928-1849
Boulevard Restaurant Mission St., 415-543-6084
Bruno's 2389 Mission St., 415-643-5200
Buena Vista Cafe 2765 Hyde St., 415-474-5044
Burma Super Star 309 Clement St., 415-387-2147.
Cafe Abir 1300 Fulton St., 415-567-7654
Café Bastille 22 Belden Place, 415-986-5673
Cafe Flore 2298 Market St., 415-621-8579
Caffe Macaroni 59 Columbus Ave., 415-956-9737
Caffè Trieste 601 Vallejo St., 415-392-6739
Capp's Corner 1600 Powell St., 415-989-2589
Cliff House 1090 Point Lobos Ave., 415-386-3330
Danilo Bakery 516 Green St., 415-989-1806
Elite Cafe 2049 Fillmore St., 415-346-8668
Enrico's 504 Broadway; 415-982-6223
Farallon 450 Post St., 415-956-6969
Fisherman's Grotto No 9 9 Fisherman's Wharf, 415-673-7025
Fog City Diner 1300 Battery St., 415-982-2000
Foreign Cinema 534 Mission St., 415-648-7600
Golden Era Vegetarian Restaurant 572 O'Farrell St., 415-673-3136
Golden Gate Fortune Cookie Company 56 Ross Alley, 415-781-3956

Grand Cafe 501 Geary St., 415-292-0101

Greens Fort Mason Center, Building A, 415-771-6222

House of Shields 39 New Montgomery St., 415-392-7732

Jackson Fillmore 2506 Fillmore St., 415-346-5288

Julius' Castle 1541 Montgomery St., 415-392-2222

Kabuto Sushi 5121 Geary Blvd., 415-752-5652

Kan Zaman 1793 Haight St., 415-751-9656

La Palma Mexica-tessen 2884 24th St., 415-647-1500

La Taquería 2889 Mission St., 415-285-7117

Lefty O'Doul's 333 Geary St., 415-982-8900

Liberty Cafe 10 Cortland Ave., 415-695-8777

Liguria 1700 Stockton St., 415-421-3786

Lime 2247 Market St., 415-621-5256

Louis' Restaurant 902 Point Lobos Ave., 415-387-6330

Magnolia Pub & Brewery 1398 Haight St., 415-864-7468

Medjool 2522 Mission St., 415-550-9055

Minh's Garden 208 Clement St., 415-751-8211

Moki's Sushi and Pacific Grill 615 Cortland Ave., 415-970-9336

Molinari Delicatessen 373 Columbus Ave., 415-421-2337

Moose's 1652 Stockton St., 415-989-7800

Original Joe's 144 Taylor St., 415-775-4877

Pier 23 Cafe Pier 23, 415-362-5125

Pine Crest Diner 401 Geary St., 415-885-6407

Plouf 40 Belden Place, 415-986-6491

Postrio 545 Post St., 415-776-7825

Quince Restaurant 1701 Octavia St., 415-775-8500

Red's Java House Pier 30, 415-777-5626

Rose Pistola 532 Columbus Ave., 415-399-0499

Sam's Grill 374 Bush St., 415-421-0594

Sears' Fine Foods 439 Powell St., 415-986-0700

Slanted Door 1 Ferry Building, 415-861-8032

St. Francis Fountain 2801 24th St., 415-826-4200

Tadich Grill 240 California St., 415-391-1849

Tad's Steaks 120 Powell St., 415-982-1718

Taquería Can-Cun 2288 Mission St., 415-252-9560
Tommy's Mexican Restaurant 5929 Geary Blvd., 415-387-4747
Ton Kiang 5821 Geary Blvd., 415-386-8530
Toy Boat Dessert Cafe 401 Clement St., 415-751-7505
Warming Hut Crissy Field
Yank Sing 101 Spear St., 415-957-9300

HOTELS

Archbishop's Mansion 1000 Fulton St., 415-563-7872
Argonaut Hotel 495 Jefferson St., 415-563-0800
Chateau Tivoli 1057 Steiner St., 415-776-5462
Fairmont Hotel 950 Mason St., 415-772-5000
Hyatt Regency 5 Embarcadero Center, 415-788-1234
Mark Hopkins Hotel 999 California St., 415-392-3434
Miyako Hotel 1625 Post St., 415-922-3200
Palace Hotel 2 New Montgomery St., 415-512-1111
Phoenix Hotel 601 Eddy St., 415-776-1380
Red Victorian B&B 1665 Haight St., 415-864-1978

ENTERTAINMENT & NIGHTLIFE

12 Galaxies 2565 Mission St., 415-970-9777
15 Romolo 15 Romolo Pl; 415-398-1359
222 Club 222 Hyde St., 415-440-0222
Atlas Cafe 3049 20th St., 415-648-1047
Aunt Charlie's Lounge 133 Turk St., 415-441-2922
Bimbo's 365 Club 1025 Columbus Ave., 415-474-0365
Boom Boom Room 1601 Fillmore St., 415-673-8000
C. Bobby's Owl Tree 601 Post St., 415-776-9344
Cafe Du Nord 2170 Market St., 415-861-5016
Castro Theater 429 Castro St., 415-621-6120
Doc's Clock 2575 Mission St., 415-824-3627

Edinburgh Castle 950 Geary St., 415-885-4074

Elbo Room 647 Valencia St., 415-552-7788

Fillmore Auditorium 1805 Geary Blvd., 415-346-6000

Gangway 841 Larkin St., 415-776-6828

Gino and Carlo 548 Green St; 415-421-0896

Gold Dust Lounge 247 Powell St., 415-397-1695

Great American Music Hall 859 O'Farrell St., 415-885-0750

Ha Ra 875 Geary St., 415-673-3148

Hi Dive Pier 28-1/2, 415-977-0170

Latin American Club 3286 22nd St., 415-647-2732

Lusty Lady 1033 Kearny St., 415-391-3991

Makeout Room 3225 22nd St., 415-2888

Mario's Bohemian Cigar Store 566 Columbus Ave; 415-362-0536

Mint Karaoke Lounge 1942 Market St., 415-626-4726

Mitchell Bros. O'Farrell Theater 895 O'Farrell St., 415-776-6686

Old Ship Saloon 298 Pacific Ave., 415-788-2222

Perry's 1944 Union St., 415-922-9022

Pied Piper Bar 2 New Montgomery St., 415-512-1111

Plough and the Stars 116 Clement St., 415-751-1122

Purple Onion 140 Columbus Ave., 415-956-1610

Rite Spot 2099 Folsom St., 415-552-6066

Saloon 1232 Grant Ave; live music cover $2-5; 415-989-7666

San Francisco Brewing Company 155 Columbus Ave., 415-434-3344

Specs' 12 William Saroyan Place; 415-421-4112

Starlight Room 450 Powell St., 415-395-8595

Tonga Room 950 Mason St., 415-772-5278

Tony Nik's 1534 Stockton St; 415-693-0993

Top of the Mark 999 California St., 415-616-6916

Tosca Cafe 242 Columbus Ave; 415-391-1244

Trad'r Sam 6150 Geary Blvd., 415-221-0773

Tunnel Top 601 Bush St., 415-986-8900

Twin Peaks Tavern 401 Castro St., 415-864-9470

Uptown 200 Capp St., 415-861-8231

Vesuvio 255 Columbus Ave; 415-362-3370

Wild Side West 424 Cortland Ave., 415-647-3099
Zeitgeist 199 Valencia St., 415-255-7505

MUSEUMS & GALLERIES

111 Minna St. Gallery 111 Minna St., 415-974-1719
Asian Art Museum 200 Larkin St., 415-581-3500
Beat Museum 540 Broadway, 800-537-6822
Cable Car Museum 1201 Mason St., 415-474-1887
California Historical Society 678 Mission St., 415-357-1848 (closed Sunday–Tuesday)
Cartoon Art Museum 655 Mission St., 415-227-8666 (closed Monday)
Galería de la Raza 2857 24th St., 415-826-8009
M.H. De Young Memorial Museum 50 Hagiwara Tea Garden Dr., 415-863-3330
Museum of Craft and Folk Art 51 Yerba Buena Lane, 415-227-4888
Museum of the African Diaspora 685 Mission St., 415-358-7200 (closed Tuesday)
Palace of the Legion of Honor Lincoln Park, 34th Ave. and Clement St., 415-863-3330
San Francisco Arts Commission Gallery 401 Van Ness Ave., 415-554-6080
San Francisco National Maritime Museum 900 Beach St., 415- 561-7100
SFMoMA 151 Third St., 415-357-4000
The Chinese Historical Society of America 965 Clay St., 415-391-1188
Wells Fargo History Museum 420 Montgomery St., 415-396-2619
Yerba Buena Center for the Arts 701 Mission St.,

EDUCATIONAL & CULTURAL CENTERS

Exploratorium 3601 Lyon St., 415-563-7337
Hyde St. Pier 415-447-5000
Main Library 100 Larkin St., 415-557-4400
Maritime Visitor Center Hyde and Jefferson streets, 415-447-5000
Precita Eyes Art Store & Visitors Center 2981 24th St., 415-285-2287
San Francisco Art Institute 800 Chestnut St., 415-771-7020
The Center 1800 Market St., 415-865-5555

Historical Landmarks & Monuments

Bank of Canton (Old Chinese Telephone Exchange) 743 Washington St
City Club 155 Sansome St., 415-648-7198
Colonial Dames Octagon House 2645 Gough St., 415-441-7512
Masonic Memorial Temple 1111 California St., 415-776-4702
Officers' Club (NPS Visitors Center) Presidio, 415-561-4323
Redstone Building 2926 16th St.
San Francisco Columbarium 1 Loraine Court
SS *Jeremiah O'Brien* Pier 45, 415-544-0100
USS *Pampanito* Pier 45, 415-561-7006
Women's Building 3543 18th St., 415-431-1180

Places of Worship

Buddhist Church 1881 Pine St.
Grace Cathedral 1100 California St., 415-749-6300
Konko Kyo Church 1909 Bush St.
Mission Dolores 3321 16th St., 415-621-8203
Notre Dame des Victoires 566 Bush St., 415-397-0113
Sts. Peter and Paul Church 666 Filbert St., 415-421-0809
Vedanta Temple 2963 Webster St.

Shopping

A Different Light Bookstore 489 Castro St., 415-431-0891
Aria 1522 Grant Ave., 415-433-0219
Book Bay Fort Mason, Fort Mason Center, Building C, 415-771-1076
Bound Together Book Collective 1369 Haight St., 415-431-8355
Canton Bazaar 616 Grant Ave., 415-362-5750
Casa Lucas Market 2934 24th St., 415-593-0785
Chinatown Kite Shop 717 Grant Ave., 415-989-5182
Clarion Music Center 816 Sacramento St., 415-391-1317

Cliff's Variety Store 479 Castro St., 415-431-5365
Green Apple Books and Music 506 Clement St., 415-387-2272
Image Leather 2199 Market St., 415-621-7551
Kamei 525-547 Clement St., 415-666-3688
Kayo Books 814 Post St., 415-749-0554
Kinokuniya Bookstore 1581 Webster St., 415-567-7625
Marcus Books 1712 Fillmore St., 415-346-4222
Mission Market Fish & Poultry 2590 Mission St., 415-282-3331
New May Wah Supermarket 719 Clement St., 415-221-9826
Nijiya Market 1737 Post St., 415-563-1901
Pipe Dreams 1376 Haight St., 415-431-3553
Positively Haight Street 1400 Haight St., 415-252-8747
Safeway 2020 Market St., 415-861-7660
Soul Patch Tattoo and Piercing 1599 Haight St., 415-552-3444
Wasteland 1660 Haight, 415-863-3150

Parks & Gardens

Conservatory of Flowers John F. Kennedy Dr., 415-666-7001
Hagiwara Japanese Tea Garden Hagiwara Tea Garden Dr., 415-831-2700
Strybing Arboretum & Botanical Gardens 9th Avenue at Lincoln Way, 415-661-1316

Miscellaneous

AT&T Park 24 Willie Mays Plaza (corner Third and King), 415-972-1800

INDEX

aBOUT THE auTHor

Tom Downs grew up in the suburbs south of San Francisco and always felt the pull of the big city. From a very early age, skyscrapers, big-league baseball, Italian restaurants, darkly lit saloons, grand parks, museums, cramped little taquerías, the whistles of hotel doormen, the bells of trolleys, the smell of fish, the babble of languages, and the constant hush and hum of traffic and people held our author in thrall. As an adult, Tom divided a decade between Los Angeles and New York before finally moving to San Francisco. Researching this book gave him the excuse to dissect the city in a methodical manner. Tom has authored guide-books to such far-flung lands as New Orleans; the Mississippi Delta; the west of Ireland; Hanoi, Vietnam; and also our beloved San Francisco. He lived in the Mission District and in Chinatown before migrating to Oakland with his wife and kids, who are all card sharks.